GOURMET COOKING
for *ONE* or *TWO*

GOURMET COOKING
for *ONE* or *TWO*

Incredible Meals That Are
Small in Size but *Big on Flavor*

April Anderson
founder of Girl Gone Gourmet

PAGE STREET
PUBLISHING CO.

First published in 2018 by

Page Street Publishing Co.

27 Congress Street, Suite 105

Salem, MA 01970

www.pagestreetpublishing.com

Distributed by Macmillan, sales in Canada by The Canadian Manda Group.

22 21 20 19 18   1 2 3 4 5

ISBN-13: 978-1-62414-619-0

ISBN-10: 1-62414-619-8

Library of Congress Control Number: 2018935167

Cover and book design by Kylie Alexander for Page Street Publishing Co.

Photography by April Anderson, author photo on page 172 by Lister Photography

Printed and bound in China

For my mom, Suzi,
and my brothers, Bobby and Scott.

CONTENTS

Introduction

I believe cooking is one of the kindest things you can do for yourself. Chopping, simmering and stirring, transforming ingredients into a meal that you made by yourself for yourself, creates a sense of satisfaction no meal from a box or bag can deliver. But in a world where a lot of recipes are written for four or more people, those of us who want to cook for ourselves are faced with either eating the same thing for days on end or trying to scale the recipe down so that it serves one, with maybe enough leftovers for lunch the next day.

As a food blogger, I've been on both sides of the coin. Many of the recipes I develop for my blog, Girl Gone Gourmet, are of the "serves four or more" variety. But when I take my blogger hat off and it's just me in the kitchen, I cook just enough to serve myself. It's a way of cooking I've grown to love, so I wrote this book to show you how I use simple and accessible ingredients to make comfort food–inspired dinners for one or two.

The inspiration for these recipes started with the meals I shared with my family growing up in Wyoming. The food we passed around our kitchen table was honest, approachable and steeped in wholesome goodness. It's from those roots that the recipes in this book took shape, with a heavy dose of influence from my experiences living in and traveling to different places. So the recipes have a familiar feel, but with some twists—and all of them serve just one or two.

The Solo Kitchen

For a first-time solo cook, there are a few things to consider before diving into the pages of this book.

Recipes

Unlike traditional cookbooks that offer recipes for breakfast, lunch, dinner and everything in between, here you'll find dinner recipes divided into sections ranging from quick 30-minute ideas to the low and slow variety. In many cases, you'll find that within a recipe there are ingredients for making both a main dish and a side dish, so there's no need to flip back and forth to different sections in the book. Each recipe is a meal unto itself.

Ingredients

Buy only what you need. Many mainstream grocery stores have fish and meat counters where a variety of ingredients can be purchased in small amounts. For example, before buying a package of six pork chops, check the counter to see if they are sold individually. Take advantage of the scales and the pre-prepped veggie section in the produce department to buy just what you need for a given recipe.

For consistency, I used kosher salt in all of the recipes, as well as regular store-bought stocks, the salt content of which can vary from brand to brand. With that in mind, it's always a good practice to taste as you go and adjust the salt as needed.

Throughout this book some of the ingredients are repeated. In cases where buying a small amount just isn't possible, you'll notice you can use some of it in one recipe and the rest a few pages later in a completely different recipe. This means that you should be able to put to use the things you buy, though it does depend on how often you cook.

In developing and testing the recipes for this book, I got feedback from some folks for whom small-scale cooking took a little getting used to. If you're one of those people who are accustomed to making recipes that serve several people, the amounts called for in these recipes may feel really tiny, like you're cooking for a dollhouse dinner party, but rest assured that after you've cooked your way through a few recipes, it starts to feel more comfortable.

Equipment

Like the smaller-scale ingredients, smaller-scale equipment is also needed for these recipes. Each recipe specifies the size and type of pan or baking dish needed, but here is a short list of the most-used tools:

- Both a regular and a nonstick 8½-inch (22-cm) ovenproof skillet

- Both a regular and a nonstick 10-inch (25-cm) ovenproof skillet

- 2-quart (2-L) saucepan and 3½-quart (3-L) saucepan

- 20-oz (590-ml) baking dish

- Baking sheet

- An immersion (or stick) blender for pureeing hot soups

- A digital kitchen scale for measuring pasta and other ingredients

- Run-of-the-mill kitchen equipment like measuring cups and spoons, mixing bowls, graters and a sharp knife

Last but not least, I want you to enjoy yourself, because I believe time spent in the kitchen cooking for yourself is time well spent.

Updated Classics to Serve Yourself

(and Not a Crowd)

Classics are classics for a reason: they are timeless and beloved. But recipes for such endearing dishes are packaged with an assumption that they are to be shared, so they are often scaled to serve many, sometimes for a special occasion or holiday. For those of us cooking for ourselves, are we to wait for a reason to justify making our favorite time-honored dishes? I think not.

As is my way, I haven't just scaled down some favorite classic recipes, I've played around with them too. Some, like the Chicken Noodle Casserole (page 15), stay true to their humble roots with only a few tweaks here and there. Others, like the Chicken Meatballs with Spring Green Spaghetti (page 19) or the Blue Cheese Beef Enchiladas with Apple Walnut Salad (page 20), boldly venture off the beaten path.

There are a few quick and easy dishes, several that are more involved and a few in between, but all of the recipes in this chapter maintain some level of familiarity that invoke the feel-good vibes of the original classic.

Chicken Noodle Casserole

This casserole, with its tender vegetables, chicken and pasta baked in a creamy sauce, is what happens when you take the best of chicken pot pie and marry it with a classic chicken noodle casserole.

Serves 1

2 oz (60 g) penne pasta

4 tsp (20 ml) olive oil, divided

1 (4-oz [115-g]) boneless, skinless chicken breast, ½" (1.3 cm) thick

1 tsp kosher salt, plus more for seasoning

Black pepper

¼ cup (38 g) finely chopped onion

1 tsp chopped garlic

⅓ cup (37 g) diced carrot

1 tbsp (14 g) unsalted butter

1 tbsp (8 g) all-purpose flour

¾ cup (180 ml) 2% milk

2 tsp (2 g) fresh thyme leaves

¼ cup (38 g) frozen peas

1 tbsp (11 g) shredded Parmesan

1 tbsp (8 g) fine bread crumbs

Preheat the oven to 350°F (175°C). Boil the pasta for half the amount of time listed on the package, drain it and set it aside.

In an 8½-inch (22-cm) skillet, heat 2 teaspoons (10 ml) of olive oil over medium heat. Season the chicken with salt and pepper, place it in the pan and cook it on both sides for 3 to 4 minutes, or until it's cooked through. Turn off the heat and let the pan cool before you move on to the next step. Transfer the chicken to a cutting board and shred it into bite-size pieces.

In the same pan, heat 1 teaspoon of olive oil over medium heat. Add the onion, garlic and carrot and cook them for 5 minutes, or until they start to soften. Add the 1 teaspoon of salt and the butter and stir until the butter has melted. Sprinkle the flour over the top of the vegetables and stir until the vegetables are coated. Slowly pour the milk into the pan, stirring continuously, until the mixture is smooth. Add the thyme, shredded chicken and peas and stir. Adjust the heat to maintain a low simmer. Cook the mixture for 5 to 10 minutes, or until it starts to thicken.

Add the pasta to the pan and stir to combine. Transfer it all to a 20-ounce (590-ml) baking dish. In a small bowl, combine the cheese, bread crumbs and the remaining 1 teaspoon of olive oil. Sprinkle the bread crumb mixture over the top of the casserole. Bake the casserole for 30 minutes, uncovered, or until it's bubbling around the edges. Rest the casserole for a few minutes before serving.

Spinach Salad Steak Tacos

Inspired by a classic spinach salad with warm bacon vinaigrette, these steak tacos are an easy way to eat more veggies. The recipe makes two large-size tacos to feed one hungry person. To save half, store the leftover components separately in the fridge to assemble for lunch or dinner the next day.

Serves 1

1 slice thick-cut bacon

6 oz (170 g) sirloin steak, seasoned with salt on both sides

¼ tsp Dijon mustard

¼ tsp balsamic vinegar

1 pinch of salt

1 pinch of black pepper

2 cups (60 g) roughly chopped spinach

2 large white mushrooms, sliced

2 (8" [20-cm]) flour tortillas, charred in a dry pan

¼ cup (33 g) crumbled feta cheese

6 thin slices red onion

In an 8½-inch (22-cm) skillet, cook the bacon over medium heat until it's crispy, about 2 to 3 minutes per side. Transfer the bacon to a small plate lined with a paper towel and set it aside. Transfer half of the bacon fat from the skillet to a medium-size bowl, leaving the extra fat in the pan.

Adjust the heat to medium-high. Cook the steak on one side for 5 minutes. Turn it over and cook on the other side for 5 minutes. Turn the heat off and cover the pan while you make the spinach salad.

Whisk the reserved bacon fat with the mustard, vinegar, salt and pepper until combined. Add the spinach and mushrooms to the bowl and toss them with the dressing.

Transfer the steak from the skillet to a cutting board. Slice it against the grain into ¼-inch (6-mm) slices. Roughly chop the bacon for garnish. To assemble the tacos, divide the spinach salad between the flour tortillas. Top each with the steak, feta cheese, bacon and a few slices of red onion.

Chicken Meatballs *with* Spring Green Spaghetti

This dish is all about lightness. The simple green pea sauce with fresh herbs and lemon cooks fast and is a wonderful accompaniment to the savory chicken meatballs. Top the pasta and meatballs with some crispy bacon and cheese for a spring-inspired twist on traditional spaghetti and meatballs.

Serves 1

Sauce
¾ cup (114 g) frozen green peas, thawed

1 large clove garlic, roughly chopped

¼ cup (38 g) roughly chopped yellow onion

2 tsp (2 g) finely sliced fresh chives

1 tbsp (2.5 g) chopped fresh parsley

Juice of 1 lemon

¼ tsp kosher salt

⅓ cup (80 ml) water, as needed

Meatballs
1 tsp mayonnaise

1 tsp 2% milk

¼ tsp garlic powder

½ tsp kosher salt

1 pinch of black pepper

1 tsp fine bread crumbs

4 oz (115 g) ground chicken

1 slice thick-cut bacon

For Serving
2 oz (60 g) spaghetti, cooked according to package directions

2 tbsp (30 ml) reserved pasta water, as needed

1 tbsp (11 g) grated Asiago cheese

To make the sauce, place the peas, garlic, onion, chives, parsley, lemon juice and salt in a blender. Cover and puree, adding up to ⅓ cup (80 ml) of water to thin it to a sauce-like consistency. Set the sauce aside.

To make the meatballs, combine the mayonnaise, milk, garlic powder, salt, pepper and bread crumbs in a medium-size bowl. Add the chicken and use your hands to mix the ingredients just until combined. Divide the meatball mixture into 4 equal parts and roll each into a ball.

In an 8½-inch (22-cm) skillet, cook the bacon until it renders its fat and is crispy, about 2 to 3 minutes on each side. Transfer the bacon to a plate lined with a paper towel and leave the fat in the pan. Place the meatballs in the pan and brown them in the bacon fat over medium heat, turning them every 2 to 3 minutes until they are browned on all sides. While the meatballs cook, finely chop the bacon and set it aside for garnish.

Once the meatballs are browned, add the sauce to the pan and stir to coat the meatballs. Bring the sauce to a simmer and cook the meatballs until they are cooked through and the sauce has thickened, about 5 minutes. Add the cooked spaghetti to the pan and toss to coat in the sauce. Add up to 2 tablespoons (30 ml) of the reserved pasta water as needed to thin the sauce to the desired consistency. Serve the meatballs and pasta with the bacon and cheese sprinkled on top.

Blue Cheese Beef Enchiladas *with* Apple Walnut Salad

Some things are just meant to go together, and one of my favorite combos is beef and blue cheese. These decadent enchiladas have a rich blue cheese sauce that contrasts with pops of bright flavor from the apple that's in both the enchiladas and the fresh spinach salad served on the side. The recipe makes three enchiladas that easily stretch for two meals, so save the leftovers to reheat the next day.

Serves 2

Enchiladas
1 tsp olive oil

4 oz (115 g) ground beef

¼ cup (38 g) finely diced yellow onion

1 tsp minced garlic

1 cup (151 g) finely diced Granny Smith apple

½ tsp kosher salt

¼ tsp dried oregano

½ tbsp (7 g) unsalted butter

½ tbsp (4 g) all-purpose flour

½ cup (120 ml) 2% milk

½ cup (56 g) crumbled blue cheese, divided

3 (8" [20-cm]) flour tortillas

Salad
1 tbsp (15 ml) olive oil

2 tsp (10 ml) apple cider vinegar

1 pinch of kosher salt

1 pinch of black pepper

4 cups (120 g) roughly chopped spinach

½ cup (90 g) thinly sliced Granny Smith apple

2 tbsp (16 g) chopped walnuts

Preheat the oven to 350°F (175°C).

To make the enchiladas, heat the olive oil in an 8½-inch (22-cm) skillet over medium heat. Add the ground beef and cook for 3 to 4 minutes until it's no longer pink, using a spatula to break it up as it cooks. Add the onion, garlic, apple, salt and oregano. Stir and cook for 2 to 3 minutes, or until the onion has softened. Transfer the beef mixture to a clean plate and set aside.

In the same skillet, melt the butter over medium-low heat. Add the flour and stir to combine it with the butter. Slowly add the milk, stirring continuously, until smooth. Cook for 5 minutes, adjusting the heat to keep it from boiling, until it starts to thicken. Add ¼ cup (28 g) of the cheese and stir for 2 to 3 minutes until it's melted into the milk and the sauce is thick enough to coat the back of a spoon.

To assemble the enchiladas, divide the beef mixture evenly among the tortillas. Roll the tortillas and place them seam-side down in a 20-ounce (590-ml) baking dish. Pour the cheese sauce over the top of the tortillas, cover the dish with foil and transfer it to the oven. Bake the enchiladas for 20 minutes, or until they are hot and bubbling.

While the enchiladas bake, assemble the salad. Whisk the olive oil, vinegar, salt and pepper in a medium-size bowl. Add the spinach and lightly toss it in the dressing until it's evenly coated. Add the apple and walnuts and toss again to combine. Serve with the enchiladas, garnished with the remaining ¼ cup (28 g) blue cheese.

Chicken Fritters *with* Corn Salad

It's hard not to eat these fritters straight from the pan—each crispy bite has a touch of pepper Jack cheese and buttermilk-battered chicken. But taking a few minutes to make the cold corn salad with bell pepper, fresh cilantro and simple sour cream dressing takes what might otherwise be just an appetizer and makes it dinner.

Serves 1

Salad
½ cup (83 g) frozen corn

⅓ cup (60 g) finely diced red bell pepper

1 tbsp (9 g) chopped red onion

¼ cup (8 g) thinly sliced baby spinach

Juice of ½ lime

1 tsp chopped cilantro

1 pinch of kosher salt

Dressing
2 tbsp (15 g) sour cream

Juice of ½ lime

1 pinch of salt

Fritters
2 tbsp (16 g) all-purpose flour

¼ tsp garlic powder

¼ tsp dried oregano

¼ tsp kosher salt

1 pinch of black pepper

2 tbsp (30 ml) buttermilk

1 (4-oz [115-g]) boneless, skinless chicken breast, finely chopped

¼ cup (33 g) grated pepper Jack cheese

1 tsp chopped fresh cilantro

2 tsp (10 ml) vegetable oil

To make the salad, combine the corn, bell pepper, onion, spinach, lime juice, cilantro and salt in a medium-size bowl and set aside. There's no need to thaw the frozen corn first; in the time it takes to prepare and cook the fritters, the corn will have thawed.

To make the dressing, combine the sour cream, lime juice and salt in a small-size bowl and set aside.

To make the fritters, combine the flour, garlic powder, dried oregano, salt, pepper, buttermilk, chicken, cheese and cilantro in a medium-size bowl. In a 10-inch (25-cm) nonstick skillet, heat the oil over medium-high heat. Scoop half of the chicken mixture and place it in the pan. Press down on it with a spatula to form a patty approximately ¼ inch (6 mm) thick. Repeat with the other half of the chicken mixture. Adjust the heat to medium and cook the fritters for 2 to 3 minutes on each side until they are golden brown. Transfer the fritters to a plate lined with a paper towel.

To serve, spoon the corn salad onto a plate with the fritters on the side. Drizzle the sour cream dressing over the top or use it as a dipping sauce for the fritters.

Creamy Pumpkin Spinach Fettuccine

If you've only ever thought of pumpkin as an ingredient used in desserts, then this pasta might seem a little strange. But I can promise that it deserves a place in your savory recipe repertoire, and there's no better way to give it a try than in a creamy pasta dish. The sauce starts as a basic Alfredo to which the pumpkin and spinach are added. From there, just toss the sauce with the hot pasta and dinner is served.

Serves 2

2 tbsp (28 g) unsalted butter

1 large clove garlic, smashed

¼ cup (60 ml) heavy cream

¼ cup (60 g) pumpkin puree

¼ tsp kosher salt

¼ cup (40 g) frozen chopped spinach

¼ cup (45 g) shredded Parmesan cheese, plus 1 tsp for garnish

3 oz (85 g) fettuccine, cooked according to package directions

2 tbsp (30 ml) reserved pasta water, as needed

1 tsp chopped fresh parsley, for garnish

In an 8½-inch (22-cm) skillet, melt the butter over medium-low heat. Add the garlic and cook for 1 to 2 minutes, or until fragrant. Add the cream and adjust the heat to medium. Whisk the butter and cream together until combined. Discard the garlic.

Add the pumpkin and salt and stir until combined. Add the spinach and stir for 2 to 3 minutes until it's thawed and warmed through. Add ¼ cup (45 g) of the cheese and stir for 1 to 2 minutes until it melts and the sauce is smooth. Add the cooked pasta and toss it in the sauce until it's evenly coated. If needed, add up to 2 tablespoons (30 ml) of the reserved pasta water to thin the sauce. Sprinkle the parsley and remaining 1 teaspoon of cheese over the top of the pasta to garnish.

Strawberry Balsamic Oven Ribs
with Potato Salad

These tender oven ribs, coated in spices and brushed with a sweet and tangy sauce, made with fresh strawberries and balsamic vinegar, require two things: time and patience. Your effort will be well rewarded when you help yourself to a serving of ribs with a scoop of creamy potato salad on the side.

Serves 2

Ribs
1 (3-lb [1.3-kg]) rack baby back pork ribs

2 tsp (10 g) kosher salt

1 tbsp (8 g) chili powder

1 tsp brown sugar

1 tsp paprika

1 tsp onion powder

1 tsp garlic powder

1 tsp dried oregano

½ tsp ground black pepper

Potato Salad
12 oz (340 g) Yukon gold potatoes, cut into 1" (2.5-cm) pieces

¼ cup (55 g) mayonnaise

2 tsp (10 g) Dijon mustard

1 tbsp (3 g) chopped fresh parsley

Salt and black pepper

Sauce
2 tsp (10 ml) olive oil

¼ cup (38 g) chopped red onion

3 cloves garlic, chopped

8 oz (225 g) strawberries, stems removed and quartered

¼ tsp crushed red pepper flakes

1 tbsp (13 g) brown sugar

Juice of 1 lemon

1 tbsp (15 ml) balsamic vinegar

1 tsp kosher salt

Preheat the oven to 300°F (150°C). Line a baking sheet with foil and place a wire baking rack in the center.

To make the ribs, first turn them meat-side down on a cutting board. Using the tip of a knife, loosen a part of the thin membrane that runs along the length of the ribs. Once you've separated a couple of inches, hold the membrane and pull to remove it from the ribs. Discard the membrane.

In a small bowl, combine the kosher salt, chili powder, brown sugar, paprika, onion powder, garlic powder, dried oregano and pepper. Rub the mixture all over the ribs and place on the baking sheet. Cover with another sheet of foil, leaving space around the ribs so the heat can circulate. Transfer to the oven and bake for 3½ hours.

To make the potato salad, place the potatoes in a 3½-quart (3-L) saucepan and cover them with cold water. Bring to a boil and cook for 10 minutes. Meanwhile, combine the mayonnaise, mustard, parsley and salt and pepper to taste in a medium-size bowl. Drain the potatoes, spread them in an even layer on a baking sheet and cool them to room temperature. Transfer the cooled potatoes to the bowl with the dressing and gently stir until evenly coated. Cover the bowl with plastic and refrigerate until ready to serve.

To make the sauce, heat the olive oil in a 3½-quart (3-L) saucepan. Add the olive oil, red onion, garlic, strawberries, red pepper flakes, brown sugar, lemon juice, balsamic vinegar and salt. Stir and bring the mixture to a simmer. Cook the sauce for 10 to 12 minutes, or until the strawberries have broken down and released their juices and the mixture is thickened.

Place a fine-mesh strainer over a medium-size bowl. Pour the sauce into the strainer and, using a spatula, press on the solids to extract all of the liquid. Discard the solids and place the sauce in the refrigerator.

Once the ribs have baked for 3½ hours, uncover them and brush half the sauce over the top of the ribs. Return them to the oven for 15 minutes. Repeat with the remaining sauce and bake them for 15 minutes, or until the internal temperature is 190°F (88°C) and the meat easily pulls away from the bone. Let the ribs rest for 5 minutes on the baking sheet. To slice, run the knife in between the bones to separate the ribs. Serve with the potato salad.

Chicken *with* Red Wine Sauce *and* Cauliflower Mash

Inspired by the French bistro favorite coq au vin, this chicken dish with a velvety red wine sauce and side of Parmesan cauliflower mash won't take you all day to make but delivers the same comforting coziness.

Serves 1

Chicken and Sauce
2 bone-in, skin-on chicken thighs, seasoned with salt on both sides

1 tbsp (8 g) all-purpose flour

1 slice thick-cut bacon, cut into ½" (1.3-cm) pieces

1 tbsp (14 g) unsalted butter

¼ cup (38 g) finely diced yellow onion

½ cup (60 g) diced carrot

1 tsp minced garlic

1 tsp tomato paste

¼ tsp kosher salt

¼ tsp black pepper

1 tsp fresh thyme leaves

2 tsp (2 g) chopped fresh parsley

½ cup (120 ml) pinot noir wine, divided

½ cup (120 ml) chicken stock

Cauliflower
2 tsp (10 ml) olive oil

6 oz (170 g) fresh cauliflower florets, roughly chopped

1 cup (235 ml) water

1 tbsp (14 g) unsalted butter

2 tbsp (22 g) grated Parmesan cheese

¼ tsp kosher salt

2 tsp (2 g) chopped fresh parsley

Preheat the oven to 350°F (175°C).

To make the chicken, coat the seasoned chicken in the flour; set aside.

In an oven-safe 3-quart (3-L) saucepan, cook the bacon over medium heat until it has rendered its fat, 2 to 3 minutes per side. Push the bacon to the side of the pan and place the chicken, skin-side down, in the bacon fat. Cook the chicken until the skin is browned, about 10 minutes. Transfer the chicken to a clean plate, leaving the bacon in the pan.

In the same pan, melt the butter over medium heat. Add the onion, carrot and garlic. Stir to coat the vegetables in the butter. Add the tomato paste, stirring until it evenly coats the vegetables. Add the salt, pepper, thyme and parsley. Add ¼ cup (60 ml) of the wine to the pan, scraping up the browned bits off the bottom of the pan as it simmers. Add the remaining ¼ cup (60 ml) wine and the chicken stock and stir to combine. Place the chicken in the liquid, skin-side up. Cover the pan with a lid slightly askew to allow steam to escape. Transfer the pan to the oven and bake until the chicken's internal temperature reaches 165°F (74°C), about 30 minutes.

Transfer the chicken to a cutting board. Strain the liquid into a medium-size bowl with a fine-mesh strainer. Discard the solids and pour the liquid back into the same pan. Bring the liquid to a boil over high heat and then reduce the heat to medium. Simmer the liquid for 5 to 10 minutes, or until it's reduced and thick enough to coat the back of a spoon. Turn off the heat, place the chicken in the sauce and cover the pan while you make the cauliflower mash.

To make the cauliflower, in an 8½-inch (22-cm) skillet, heat the olive oil over medium heat. Add the cauliflower florets and cook for 5 minutes, or until they turn golden in spots. Add the water slowly to the pan to avoid splattering, then cover and cook the florets for 5 minutes. Uncover the pan and continue simmering the florets for another 5 to 10 minutes, or until most of the liquid has evaporated and the cauliflower is fork tender. Add the butter and, once it melts, turn off the heat and mash the florets until they are creamy. Add the cheese, salt and parsley and stir to combine.

If needed, reheat the sauce and chicken over medium heat for a couple of minutes. To serve, place the cauliflower mash on a plate, top it with the chicken and spoon the sauce over the top.

Two-Slice Sun-Dried Tomato *and* Sausage Lasagna

This two-slice lasagna delivers all the comfort and good feelings of a standard-size lasagna without a pile of dishes to clean up or enough leftovers to feed a small army. This recipe only requires one skillet to make the simple white and sun-dried tomato sauces, and the oven-ready lasagna noodles go straight from the package to a loaf pan that's just the right size to bake a lasagna with two generous servings.

Serves 2

2 tsp (10 ml) olive oil

8 oz (225 g) mild Italian sausage links, casings removed

⅓ cup (50 g) finely chopped yellow onion

1 tbsp (10 g) minced garlic

1 tsp dried oregano

1 tsp kosher salt

¼ cup (40 g) chopped oil-packed sun-dried tomatoes

1 cup (235 ml) canned tomato sauce

2 tsp (2 g) chopped fresh parsley

1 tbsp (14 g) unsalted butter

1 tbsp (8 g) all-purpose flour

1 cup (235 ml) 2% milk

4 sheets flat oven-ready (no-boil) lasagna noodles

½ cup (90 g) grated Parmesan cheese

½ cup (90 g) shredded provolone cheese

Preheat the oven to 375°F (190°C).

Heat the olive oil in an 8½-inch (22-cm) skillet over medium heat. Add the sausage, breaking it up with a spatula as it cooks. Add the onion, garlic, oregano and salt and cook it with the sausage until the onions start to soften, 4 to 5 minutes. Add the tomatoes and the tomato sauce and adjust the heat to bring the sauce to a simmer. Add the parsley, stir and transfer the sauce to a bowl. Set the bowl aside while you make the white sauce.

In the same skillet, melt the butter over medium heat. Add the flour, stir and cook until it's smooth and lightly bubbling, about 2 minutes. Slowly add the milk, whisking continuously, until it's incorporated with the butter and flour. Bring the sauce to a simmer and cook, whisking frequently, until it thickens enough to coat the back of a spoon, 2 to 3 minutes.

Lightly coat the bottom of the loaf pan with ¼ cup (60 ml) of the sun-dried tomato sauce. Place a noodle in the pan and top it with ¼ cup (60 ml) of the same sauce. Drizzle ¼ cup (60 ml) of the white sauce over the top. Top with 1 tablespoon (11 g) of the Parmesan cheese and 1 tablespoon (11 g) of the provolone cheese. Start the next layer with another lasagna noodle and more of each sauce and cheese. Repeat with the remaining noodles, sauces and cheese. For the last layer, top the noodle with the remaining meat sauce, Parmesan and provolone cheese.

Cover the pan with foil and bake the lasagna for 20 minutes. Remove the foil and bake for another 10 minutes, or until the lasagna is bubbling around the edges. Let the lasagna stand for a few minutes before slicing and serving.

Turkey Chili–Topped Mashed Potatoes

Best described as pure comfort in a bowl, these mashed potatoes topped with chili are the dish to make when the weather turns cold and you need something hearty and filling. The recipe calls for ground turkey, but you can also use ground beef. I like to dress mine up with lots of garnishes, which is a great way to use up any odds and ends in the refrigerator.

Serves 1

Chili
1 slice thick-cut bacon, chopped

4 oz (115 g) ground turkey

¼ cup (38 g) finely chopped red onion

1 tsp minced garlic

1 tsp chili powder

½ tsp ground cumin

½ tsp kosher salt

¼ tsp paprika

1 tbsp (9 g) canned diced green chile

½ cup (120 ml) tomato sauce

¼ cup (60 ml) chicken stock

Mashed Potatoes
1 (8-oz [226-g]) Yukon gold potato, peeled and cut into 2" (5-cm) pieces

1 tbsp (8 g) sour cream

1 tbsp (15 ml) heavy cream

¼ tsp dried oregano

1 pinch of kosher salt

1 pinch of black pepper

Optional Garnishes
¼ cup (30 g) shredded cheddar cheese

1 green onion, sliced

1 radish, thinly sliced

1 tbsp (9 g) diced red onion

1 tbsp (8 g) sour cream

1 tsp chopped fresh cilantro

To make the chili, cook the bacon and turkey in a 2-quart (2-L) saucepan over medium heat until the turkey is no longer pink, 3 to 4 minutes. Add the onion, garlic, chili powder, cumin, salt and paprika and stir to coat the meat in the spices. Add the green chile, tomato sauce and chicken stock, adjust the heat to medium-high and bring the chili to a boil. Adjust the heat to medium and let the chili simmer and reduce for 30 minutes while you make the potatoes.

To make the mashed potatoes, place the potato pieces in a 3½-quart (3-L) saucepan and cover with cold water. Bring the water to a boil over high heat and boil the potatoes for 15 minutes, or until they're fork tender.

Drain the potatoes and return them to the pan. Add the sour cream, heavy cream, oregano, salt and pepper and use a potato masher to mash the potatoes until they are smooth. Scoop the mashed potatoes onto a plate and top with the chili and garnishes of your choosing.

Salmon Cakes *with* Garlic Dill Sauce

There are crab cakes and then there are salmon cakes, which are crab cake's richer, more satisfying cousin. You can't beat the flavor of fresh dill with salmon, but fresh parsley or basil will work well, too. To make things even easier, ask the person at the fish counter to remove the salmon skin for you when you buy it; otherwise, a sharp knife makes easy work of it at home.

Serves 1

Salmon Cakes

1 tsp mayonnaise

1 tsp fresh lemon juice

1 tsp chopped fresh dill

¼ tsp kosher salt

½ tsp all-purpose flour

2 tbsp (7 g) fresh bread crumbs (see note)

4 oz (115 g) fresh salmon fillet, skin removed and meat finely chopped

½ tbsp (7 g) unsalted butter

Sauce

1 tbsp (14 g) mayonnaise

1 tsp lemon juice

1 pinch of kosher salt

½ tsp chopped dill

For Serving

2 cups (80 g) torn green leaf lettuce, for garnish

2 lemon wedges, for serving

To make the salmon cakes, in a medium-size bowl, combine the mayonnaise, lemon juice, dill, salt and flour. Add the bread crumbs and salmon and stir just until combined. Divide the mixture into 2 equal parts and form each into a patty ¼ inch (6 mm) thick.

In a 10-inch (25-cm) nonstick skillet, melt the butter over medium heat. Place the patties in the pan and cook them for 4 to 5 minutes on each side, or until they are golden and crispy on both sides. Transfer the patties to a plate lined with a paper towel.

To make the sauce, combine the mayonnaise, lemon juice, salt and dill in a small-size bowl. To serve, place the lettuce on a serving plate and top it with the salmon cakes. Drizzle the sauce over the top. Serve with the lemon wedges.

NOTE: Fresh bread crumbs make all the difference here, so don't use store-bought bread crumbs. A single slice of stale or toasted country white bread with the crusts removed is large enough to yield the amount of bread crumbs needed. You can pulse the bread in a food processor or just use your knife to chop into crumbs approximately ⅛ inch (3 mm) in size.

Chorizo-Stuffed Pepper *with* Creamy Cilantro Dressing

This recipe calls for Mexican chorizo, which is a heavily seasoned pork sausage typically sold in casings at the grocery store. Not to be confused with Spanish chorizo, a hard sausage, Mexican chorizo is sold raw. When combined with some ground beef, garlic and cooked rice, it makes a hearty filling for bell peppers. Serve them alongside a fresh green salad and drizzle some of the dressing over the top of the peppers.

Serves 1

Peppers

3 oz (85 g) Mexican chorizo

4 oz (115 g) ground beef

½ tsp dried oregano

1 tsp minced garlic

½ cup (80 g) cooked white rice

1 large bell pepper, sliced in half lengthwise, stem and seeds removed

Dressing

2 tsp (10 ml) fresh lime juice

½ tsp chopped garlic

¼ tsp chili powder

1 pinch of kosher salt

1½ tsp (7 ml) olive oil

2 tbsp (15 g) sour cream

1 tbsp (1 g) finely chopped cilantro

For Serving

4 cups (160 g) torn green leaf lettuce

Preheat the oven to 375°F (190°C). Line a baking sheet with foil.

To make the peppers, in a medium-size bowl, combine the chorizo, beef, oregano, garlic and rice. Stuff each pepper half with the meat and rice mixture. Place the peppers on the baking sheet, cover them with foil and bake for 30 minutes. Remove the foil and bake for 10 minutes, or until the internal temperature is 160°F (71°C).

While the peppers bake, make the dressing by whisking the lime juice, garlic, chili powder, salt, olive oil, sour cream and cilantro in a medium-size bowl until smooth. Toss the lettuce with half of the dressing, reserving the other half to drizzle over the stuffed peppers before serving.

Mushroom Pancetta Bolognese

This mushroom pancetta Bolognese, unlike a traditional Bolognese, is light on the meat and doesn't require hours on the stovetop. I like to serve it tossed with bucatini—a thick pasta that's hollow on the inside—but any long pasta like spaghetti or fettuccine will work well, too.

Serves 2

4 oz (115 g) pancetta, diced

8 oz (225 g) baby portobello mushrooms, roughly chopped

¼ cup (38 g) finely diced yellow onion

2 tbsp (20 g) minced garlic

¾ cup (90 g) shredded carrot

1 tsp dried Italian herbs

½ tsp kosher salt

¼ tsp crushed red pepper flakes

2 tbsp (30 ml) dry white wine

1 tbsp (16 g) tomato paste

1 cup (242 g) crushed tomatoes

¼ cup (60 ml) water

4 oz (115 g) bucatini, cooked according to package directions

¼ cup (45 g) grated Parmesan cheese, for garnish

2 tsp (2 g) chopped fresh parsley, for garnish

In a 3½-quart (3-L) saucepan, cook the pancetta until it has released its fat, about 5 minutes. Add the mushrooms and cook them with the pancetta for 10 minutes, stirring frequently, until they have cooked down and released their moisture. Add the onion, garlic, carrot, Italian herbs, salt and red pepper flakes and cook for 5 minutes, or until the onions and carrots have started to soften.

Pour the wine into the pan and use a spatula to scrape up the browned bits off the bottom of the pan. Add the tomato paste and stir until it's combined with the vegetables. Add the tomatoes and water, stir and adjust the heat to medium-low. Simmer the sauce (it should lightly bubble) for 10 to 15 minutes.

Toss the sauce with the cooked pasta and garnish with the cheese and parsley.

Crispy Oven Chicken Drumsticks
with Pancetta Green Peas

This is how to fake fried chicken without a heavy cast-iron skillet filled with bubbling hot oil. The bread crumb–coated chicken comes out of the oven hot and crispy on the outside and tender and juicy on the inside thanks to a buttermilk marinade. Plan to marinate the chicken for several hours before baking. Make the quick and easy pancetta green peas while the chicken rests and serve them on the side.

Serves 1

Chicken

½ cup (120 ml) buttermilk

1 tsp chopped fresh parsley

1 tsp fresh thyme leaves

1 clove garlic, smashed

½ tsp paprika

3 chicken drumsticks (about ¾ lb [340 g])

3 tbsp (23 g) fine bread crumbs

3 tbsp (23 g) panko bread crumbs

½ tsp dried oregano

½ tsp salt

¼ tsp black pepper

1 tsp lemon zest

Peas

2 oz (60 g) diced pancetta

½ cup (76 g) frozen green peas

Juice from ½ lemon

½ tbsp (7 g) unsalted butter

1 tsp chopped fresh parsley

To make the chicken, combine the buttermilk, parsley, thyme, garlic and paprika in a resealable bag. Add the chicken, seal the bag and smush it around to coat the chicken. Marinate the chicken in the refrigerator for 4 to 8 hours.

Preheat the oven to 425°F (220°C). Place a baking rack on a large baking sheet.

Combine the bread crumbs, panko, oregano, salt, pepper and lemon zest in a large resealable bag. Remove the chicken from the buttermilk and let the excess drip off before transferring the drumsticks to the bag with the bread crumbs. Seal the bag and then give it a few shakes to coat the chicken in the bread crumbs. Transfer the drumsticks to the wire rack on the baking sheet. Bake the chicken for 30 minutes, then turn it over and bake it for another 30 minutes, or until the internal temperature is 165°F (74°C). Remove the chicken from the oven and let it rest while you make the pancetta green peas.

To make the peas, cook the pancetta in a small saucepan over medium heat until it releases its fat and starts to turn crispy. Add the frozen peas and lemon juice. Stir until the peas are warmed through, about 5 minutes, and then add the butter and parsley. Once the butter has melted, serve the pancetta green peas with the chicken.

Deviled Egg Shrimp Rolls

This is my way of taking a favorite appetizer and turning it into dinner by adding shrimp and crisp lettuce and tucking it all into a toasted roll. Add some potato chips on the side and you get a low-maintenance, warm-weather dinner that's a whole lot easier than making a batch of deviled eggs.

Serves 1

1 large egg

2 tbsp (28 g) mayonnaise

1 tsp Dijon mustard

1 tsp chopped fresh parsley

1 pinch of kosher salt

1 pinch of black pepper

½ tsp paprika

4 oz (115 g) cooked shrimp

2 top-sliced hot dog buns, split open and lightly toasted

2 leaves green leaf lettuce

Place the egg in a 2-quart (2-L) saucepan and cover with cold water. Bring the water to a boil over high heat, then turn off the heat, cover the pan with a lid and let it sit for 10 minutes. Drain off the hot water and fill the pan with cold water and a handful of ice cubes to cool the egg.

In a small bowl, mix the mayonnaise, mustard, parsley, salt, pepper and paprika until well combined. Peel the cooled egg, roughly chop it and add it to the mayonnaise and seasonings. Add the shrimp and stir well to combine. Line the buns with a lettuce leaf and top them with the salad.

Summer Squash Tortellini Bake

Fresh herbs and roasted yellow squash pair with cheese tortellini to make a creamy sauce. I like to simmer the onion and garlic in the goat cheese sauce and then remove them before adding the pasta so the sauce is creamy smooth and subtly flavored.

Serves 2

Squash
2 cups (226 g) diced yellow squash, cut into ¼" (6-mm) pieces

2 tsp (10 ml) olive oil

½ tsp kosher salt

Sauce
2 tbsp (28 g) unsalted butter

2 tbsp (16 g) all-purpose flour

1 cup (235 ml) 2% milk

1 (2-oz [57-g]) onion wedge

4 cloves garlic, smashed

¼ tsp kosher salt

2 oz (60 g) goat cheese, crumbled

¼ tsp black pepper

2 large basil leaves, rolled and sliced into thin ribbons

9 oz (255 g) fresh cheese tortellini

¼ cup (45 g) grated Parmesan cheese

Preheat the oven to 425°F (220°C).

To make the squash, spread the squash in an even layer on a baking sheet. Drizzle the oil and sprinkle the salt over the top, then stir the squash around to coat it. Roast the squash for 20 minutes, or until it starts to turn golden and is caramelized. Remove it from the oven and lower the temperature to 350°F (175°C).

To make the sauce, melt the butter in a 2-quart (2-L) saucepan over medium heat. Add the flour and stir until it forms a loose paste. Slowly add the milk, whisking continuously, until the milk is combined with the flour and butter and there are no lumps. Lower the heat to medium-low and add the onion, garlic and salt. Cook the sauce for 10 minutes, stirring occasionally. Adjust the heat if needed to prevent it from boiling.

When the sauce lightly coats the back of a spoon, remove and discard the onion and garlic. Add the goat cheese and stir until it melts into the sauce, 2 to 3 minutes. Add the black pepper and basil.

Place the uncooked tortellini and roasted squash in a 1½-quart (1.4-L) baking dish. Pour the sauce over the pasta and squash and stir to coat them. Top the tortellini with the Parmesan cheese, cover the dish with foil and bake for 15 minutes. Remove the foil and bake for another 10 minutes, or until it's hot and bubbling.

Scaled-Down Comfort Food

My roots are in comfort food. Savory and hearty dishes are often more powerful than an album filled with faded photos in summoning feel-good memories from the past. These are the dishes that I turn to when I'm feeling nostalgic for a taste of something that doesn't just fill me up, but also brings me closer to a time and place that's long past.

These recipes bring a sense of "home" to the dinner table. But my old comfort food favorites have changed over the years after living in different places and traveling to new ones. The recipes evolved to incorporate new tastes and new ways of cooking. Sometimes it's as simple as taking an old favorite and scaling it down to fill just one plate, like the Tarragon Chicken with Roasted Parmesan Green Beans (page 72). Other times it's taking the memory of a flavor combination, like sausage and horseradish, and using it to make something new, like the Kielbasa with Creamy Horseradish Pasta (page 76).

You don't have to wait for the right occasion or enough people around the table to make these recipes. Each is a small snapshot that taps into nostalgia without lasting for days in the refrigerator.

Creamy Lemon Chicken Ziti

I love how fresh lemon brightens an otherwise rich and heavy cream sauce. Toss in some chicken, broccolini and pasta and you get a comforting dinner that doesn't take long to make. Because you cook the chicken and broccolini first, the sauce picks up all the flavors they leave behind in the pan and gives it extra layers that make it seem like it cooked longer than it really did. If you don't have broccolini on hand, a cup (91 g) of broccoli florets is a good substitution.

Serves 1

2 tbsp (28 g) unsalted butter

4 oz (115 g) boneless, skinless chicken breast, cut into bite-size pieces

4 oz (115 g) broccolini, stems trimmed

1 tsp minced garlic

Juice of 1 lemon

¼ cup (60 ml) heavy cream

1 tsp lemon zest

½ tsp kosher salt

1 pinch of black pepper

2 oz (60 g) ziti, cooked according to package directions

2 tbsp (30 ml) reserved pasta water

1 tsp sliced fresh basil, for garnish

1 tbsp (11 g) grated Parmesan or Asiago cheese, for garnish

In an 8½-inch (22-cm) skillet, melt the butter over medium heat. Add the chicken and cook until it's cooked through, about 5 minutes. Transfer the chicken to a clean plate. Place the broccolini and garlic in the same pan. Add the lemon juice and stir to coat the broccolini. Cover the pan and cook the broccolini for 5 minutes, or until it's tender. Transfer the broccoli to the plate with the chicken.

In the same pan, combine the cream, zest, salt and pepper. Bring it to a light simmer and cook it for 1 to 2 minutes, just until it starts to thicken. Add the chicken, broccolini and cooked pasta to the pan and stir to coat it all in the sauce. If needed, add up to 2 tablespoons (30 ml) of reserved pasta water to thin the sauce. Garnish with the basil and cheese.

Black Bean Skillet Nachos

During my college days I called a plate of nachos "dinner" more times than I like to admit. These days they're more of a special treat than a go-to dinner, but when a craving for bar food hits, this is how I do nachos for one: a small skillet filled with chips and topped with black beans and a simple cheese sauce.

Serves 1

Black Beans

1 tsp olive oil

2 tbsp (25 g) minced red onion

1 tbsp (9 g) canned diced green chile

½ cup (120 g) drained and rinsed canned black beans

1 pinch of kosher salt

½ tsp chili powder

½ tsp ground cumin

½ cup (120 ml) chicken stock

Juice of ½ lime

Cheese Sauce

½ cup (65 g) shredded pepper Jack cheese

¼ tsp cornstarch

¼ cup (60 ml) heavy cream

For the Nachos

Tortilla chips

2 tbsp (16 g) shredded pepper Jack cheese

1 tsp chopped fresh cilantro

1 tbsp (8 g) sour cream, for garnish (optional)

To make the black beans, heat the olive oil over medium heat in a 2-quart (2-L) saucepan. Add the onion and green chile and cook them in the oil for 2 to 3 minutes. Add the black beans, salt, chili powder and cumin. Stir to coat the beans in the spices. Add the chicken stock and lime juice and adjust the heat to bring the stock to a simmer. Simmer the black beans for 5 minutes. Mash some of the beans with a fork and simmer for 4 to 5 minutes, or until the sauce has thickened. Transfer the black beans to a clean bowl and set aside.

To make the cheese sauce, combine the cheese with the cornstarch in a small bowl. In the same pan that you used to make the black beans, heat the cream over medium-low heat for 1 minute. Add the cheese with the cornstarch and stir continuously until the cheese has melted and the sauce is creamy and thick enough to coat the back of a spoon, 1 to 2 minutes.

To assemble the nachos, place a single layer of tortilla chips in an 8½-inch (22-cm) oven-safe skillet. Spoon half of the black beans over the top of the chips followed by half of the cheese sauce. Add another layer of chips and top them with the rest of the black beans and cheese sauce. Sprinkle the pepper Jack cheese and cilantro over the top of the nachos. Transfer the skillet to the oven and place it under the broiler. Broil the nachos for 3 to 5 minutes, or until the shredded cheese has melted and the nachos are warmed through. Serve with the sour cream, if using.

Balsamic Pot Roast

In the pantheon of comfort food favorites, pot roast reigns supreme as a go-to Sunday supper to serve a crowd. To make it for two, you don't have to buy a huge cut of meat and work your way through the leftovers for days on end. Instead, look for beef packaged as stew meat, which is the same kind of beef used for pot roast but already cut into chunks and packaged in smaller amounts. By treating it as you would a bigger cut of meat—browning it before braising it with vegetables, in this case sweet parsnips and red potatoes—you get the same falling-apart-tender beef without all the leftovers.

Serves 2

2 tsp (10 ml) olive oil

1 (8-oz [225-g]) parsnip, peeled and cut into 1" (2.5-cm) pieces

½ tsp kosher salt, divided

6 oz (170 g) red potatoes, cut into 1" (2.5-cm) pieces

1 (4-oz [115-g]) yellow onion, cut into 1" (2.5-cm) pieces

8 oz (225 g) stew meat, seasoned with kosher salt

¼ cup (60 ml) balsamic vinegar

¾ cup (180 ml) beef stock

1 tsp chopped garlic

1 tsp chopped fresh thyme

2 tsp (2 g) chopped fresh parsley, for garnish

Preheat the oven to 350°F (175°C).

In an 8½-inch (22-cm) skillet, heat the olive oil over medium heat. Place the parsnip pieces in an even layer in the pan, season them with ¼ teaspoon of the salt and cook them for 2 to 3 minutes on each side, or until they are lightly golden. Transfer the parsnip to a 1½-quart (1.4-L) baking dish. In the same pan, place the potato pieces in a single layer, season with the remaining ¼ teaspoon salt and cook for 2 to 3 minutes on each side, or until they are lightly golden. Place the potatoes on top of the parsnips. Place the onions on top of the potatoes.

In the same skillet, place the beef in a single layer. Cook the meat on both sides for 2 to 3 minutes, or until it's browned. Place the meat on top of the onions in the baking dish.

Pour the balsamic into the skillet and, as it simmers, scrape up all the browned bits off the bottom of the pan. Add the beef stock, garlic and thyme and bring it to a simmer. Pour the liquid over the top of the beef in the baking dish. Cover the dish with foil and transfer it to the oven for 2 hours, or until the meat easily shreds with a fork. To serve, place some of the vegetables and beef on a plate and spoon the cooking liquid over the top. Garnish with the parsley.

Baked Eggs *in* Tomato Spinach Cream Sauce

When it's cold this baked egg dish is like a warm hug. It's a low-fuss dinner with little prep work, making it a go-to for busy nights. The eggs are baked just until their whites are set so that when you cut into the golden yolk, it adds richness to the tomato sauce. Toast up a few extra slices of bread to soak up all the sauce.

Serves 1

2 tsp (10 ml) olive oil

1 tsp minced garlic

¼ tsp dried Italian seasoning

¼ tsp red pepper flakes

½ cup (120 g) crushed tomatoes

¼ cup (60 ml) water

½ cup (15 g) chopped fresh spinach

½ tsp kosher salt, divided

2 tbsp (30 ml) heavy cream, divided

1 piece toasted bread, sliced to fit the size of the baking dish

2 large eggs

1 pinch of black pepper

1 tbsp (11 g) grated Parmesan, for garnish

1 tsp chopped fresh parsley, for garnish

Preheat the oven to 350°F (175°C).

Combine the olive oil, garlic, Italian seasoning and red pepper flakes in an 8½-inch (22-cm) skillet. Turn the heat to medium and cook the oil with the seasonings just until the garlic is fragrant, about 1 minute. Add the crushed tomatoes and water to the pan. Stir and bring the sauce to a simmer. Add the spinach and ¼ teaspoon of the salt. Cook the sauce until the spinach has wilted, 1 to 2 minutes. Add 1 tablespoon (15 ml) of the cream and stir.

Place the bread in the bottom of a 20-ounce (590-ml) baking dish. Pour the tomato cream sauce over the top. Make two shallow wells in the sauce and crack the eggs into them. Season the egg yolks with the remaining ¼ teaspoon kosher salt and the black pepper. Pour ½ tablespoon (7 ml) of the remaining cream over each egg so that it coats the yolks. Bake the eggs uncovered for 20 minutes, or until the egg whites are set. Garnish with the cheese and parsley.

Steak House Dinner

In the time it takes to roast these potatoes until they're crispy on the outside and tender on the inside, you can whip up a tender pan-seared steak with a side of creamy spinach and blue cheese. No reservations at an overpriced steak house needed.

Serves 1

Potatoes

1 (6-oz [170-g]) russet potato, cut into 1" (2.5-cm) pieces

2 tsp (10 ml) olive oil

½ tsp finely chopped fresh rosemary

1 pinch of kosher salt

1 pinch of black pepper

Cooking spray

Steak

2 tsp (10 ml) vegetable oil

1 (6-oz [170-g]) filet mignon, seasoned with kosher salt on both sides

½ tbsp (7 g) unsalted butter

Spinach

1 tbsp (14 g) unsalted butter

¼ cup (38 g) finely diced yellow onion

1 tsp minced garlic

2 cups (60 g) roughly chopped fresh spinach

2 tsp (5 g) all-purpose flour

2 tbsp (30 ml) heavy cream

1 pinch of salt

1 pinch of pepper

1 oz (28 g) blue cheese, crumbled and divided

Preheat the oven to 425°F (220°C).

To make the potatoes, toss them in a medium-size bowl with the olive oil, rosemary, salt and black pepper until they are evenly coated. Lightly coat a baking sheet with cooking spray and spread the potatoes on it in an even layer. Roast the potatoes for 20 minutes, until they are golden and crispy around the edges.

After the potatoes have roasted for 10 minutes, prepare the steak. In a 10-inch (25-cm) nonstick skillet, heat the vegetable oil over medium heat. Place the steak in the pan and sear it on one side for 6 minutes, or until a crust forms. Turn the steak and brown it on the other side for 6 minutes. Turn the steak again to sear the sides for about 30 seconds to 1 minute each. Add the butter to the pan and, once it melts, carefully tilt the pan and spoon the melted butter over the top of the steak repeatedly for about 1 minute. Transfer the steak from the pan to a cutting board and cover it loosely with foil.

While the steak rests, make the creamed spinach. In an 8½-inch (10-cm) skillet, melt the butter over medium heat. Add the onions and garlic and cook them for 2 minutes. Add the spinach and stir until it wilts and cooks down, about 1 minute. Add the flour and stir to coat the vegetables. Adjust the heat to medium-low and add the cream, salt and pepper to the pan and stir to combine. Simmer the cream until it thickens, about 1 minute. Add half of the crumbled blue cheese and stir to combine. Cover and turn off the heat.

Slice the steak against the grain into ½-inch (1.3-cm) pieces. Serve with the potatoes and creamed spinach, sprinkling the remaining cheese over the top.

Chicken Parmesan Burger
with Oven Fries

I love to take old favorites and turn them into something new, like this chicken Parmesan burger. Instead of a chicken breast topped with sauce and cheese and served with pasta, serve the chicken Parm burger style with a side of oven-roasted potato wedges.

Serves 1

Potatoes
Cooking spray

7 oz (198 g) russet potato, sliced into ½" (1.3-cm)-thick wedges

1 tsp olive oil

½ tsp kosher salt

¼ tsp black pepper

Sauce
2 tsp (10 ml) olive oil

¼ cup (60 ml) tomato sauce

½ tsp garlic powder

¼ tsp kosher salt

1 tsp chopped fresh basil

Burger
1 tbsp (8 g) bread crumbs

¼ tsp kosher salt

¼ tsp dried Italian seasoning

⌐z (142 g) ground chicken

d mozzarella

spinach,

to ribbons

Preheat the oven to 425°F (220°C). Line a baking sheet with foil and coat it lightly with cooking spray.

To make the potatoes, place the potato wedges in an even layer on the baking sheet, coat them evenly with olive oil and season them with the salt and pepper. Roast the wedges for 15 minutes, then turn them over and roast them for another 15 minutes, or until they are golden and crispy on the outside.

While the potatoes roast, prepare the sauce by heating the olive oil and tomato sauce in an 8½-inch (22-cm) nonstick skillet over medium heat until it starts to simmer. Add the garlic powder, salt and basil. Stir and simmer the sauce for 2 to 3 minutes, then transfer it to a small bowl and set it aside.

To make the burger, combine the bread crumbs, salt and Italian seasoning in a shallow bowl. Form the ground chicken into a patty ½ inch (1.3 cm) thick and coat it in the bread crumb mixture. Wipe out the skillet used to make the sauce and use it to heat the olive oil over medium heat. Cook the burger for 4 to 5 minutes on each side, or until it is cooked through. Top the burger with the cheese and cover the pan with a lid until the cheese is melted. Transfer the burger to the bun and spoon the sauce on top, along with the spinach and basil, if using. Serve with the potato wedges on the side.

Southwest Shepherd's Pie

Green chile stew meets shepherd's pie—instead of the traditional ground beef or lamb filling, this recipe has ground pork with Mexican-style beer and green chile for a Southwest twist on a comfort-food classic.

Serves 2

Filling
1 tbsp (14 g) unsalted butter

8 oz (225 g) ground pork

¼ cup (38 g) chopped red onion

1 tsp minced garlic

1 canned mild green chile, diced

½ tsp ground cumin

½ tsp kosher salt

½ tsp black pepper

2 tbsp (16 g) all-purpose flour

½ cup (120 ml) Mexican-style beer

¼ cup (60 ml) chicken stock

½ cup (83 g) frozen yellow corn kernels

Juice of ½ lime

Potatoes
12 oz (340 g) Yukon gold potatoes, peeled and cut into 1" (2.5-cm) pieces

2 tbsp (28 g) unsalted butter

¼ cup (30 g) sour cream

1 tbsp (15 ml) heavy cream

½ tsp kosher salt

¼ tsp black pepper

1 tbsp (3 g) chopped fresh cilantro, divided

To make the filling, melt the butter in an 8½-inch (22-cm) oven-safe skillet over medium heat. Add the pork, onion and garlic and cook them, breaking apart the pork as it cooks, until the pork is no longer pink, about 5 minutes. Add the green chile, cumin, salt and pepper and stir to combine. Add the flour and stir until combined.

Pour the beer into the skillet and, as it simmers, scrape up the browned bits off the bottom of the pan. Add the stock, corn and lime juice and adjust the heat to bring the liquid to a strong simmer. Adjust the heat and simmer the filling while you make the potatoes.

To make the mashed potatoes, place the potatoes in a 3½-quart (3-L) saucepan and cover them with cold water. Bring the water to a boil over high heat and boil the potatoes for 10 to 15 minutes, or until they are fork tender. Drain the potatoes and place them back in the same pan.

Add the butter, sour cream and heavy cream to the hot potatoes and use a potato masher to mash them until they are smooth. Add the salt, pepper and half of the cilantro and stir to combine.

Scoop the potatoes in a few small batches on top of the filling. Spread them with a spatula into an even layer, leaving 2 inches (5 cm) of filling exposed around the edges. Drag the tines of a fork through the potatoes to make ridges.

Preheat the broiler with the oven rack about 6 inches (15 cm) below the heating element.

Transfer the skillet to the oven and broil the tops of the potatoes until they start to turn golden in places, 3 to 5 minutes. Garnish the shepherd's pie with the remaining cilantro.

Risotto *with* Roasted Butternut Squash

Risotto is one of those dishes that has somehow gotten the reputation for being difficult to make at home, but it really isn't. All it requires is a few key ingredients and your full attention for about thirty minutes, and your time and patience will be rewarded with a plate of creamy, tender rice. Serve it with sweet roasted butternut squash for a restaurant-quality, make-at-home dinner.

This recipe makes enough for two servings, so save the leftover risotto to make Risotto Balls (page 64).

Serves 2

3 cups (705 ml) vegetable broth

2 cups (270 g) diced butternut squash, cut into 1" (2.5-cm) pieces

2 tsp (10 ml) olive oil

½ tsp kosher salt, divided

1 tbsp (14 g) unsalted butter

¼ cup (38 g) chopped yellow onion

1 tsp minced garlic

½ cup (105 g) Arborio rice

¼ cup (60 ml) dry white wine

¼ cup (30 g) shredded Asiago cheese

1 pinch of black pepper

1 tsp chopped fresh parsley, for garnish

Preheat the oven to 400°F (200°C).

While the oven preheats, warm the vegetable broth in a 3-quart (3-L) saucepan over medium-high heat until it starts to simmer. Adjust the heat to low to keep it warm.

Spread the squash in an even layer on a baking sheet. Coat the squash evenly in the oil and season it with ¼ teaspoon of the kosher salt. Roast the squash for 30 minutes while you make the risotto.

To make the risotto, melt the butter in a 2-quart (2-L) saucepan over medium heat. Add the onion and garlic and cook in the oil for 1 minute. Add the rice and stir to coat it in the butter. Add the white wine and simmer for 1 minute.

Ladle ¼ cup (60 ml) of hot vegetable stock into the pan with the rice. Stirring continuously, cook the rice in the stock until it is absorbed. Repeat this process, adding the same amount of stock each time, until you've added all the stock and the rice is tender and creamy, about 30 minutes. Once the rice is tender, add the cheese and stir until it melts into the rice. Add the remaining ¼ teaspoon of salt and stir. Serve 1 cup (200 g) of risotto with the roasted squash and garnish it with the black pepper and parsley.

Risotto Balls *with* Mixed Green Salad

If you made the Risotto with Roasted Butternut Squash (page 63) and managed not to eat it all in one sitting, this is how you put the leftovers to good use. Leftover risotto rolled into a ball, breaded and pan-fried is like a little gift to yourself. After a day in the refrigerator, the risotto will have stiffened up and will be easy to roll and bread, and after a stint in some hot oil, they'll be a crispy-on-the-outside, soft-and-rich-on-the-inside bite of goodness. In Italy, risotto balls (called *arancini*) are stuffed with cheese or finely chopped vegetables, but for our purposes we're keeping it simple.

Serves 1

Risotto Balls
1 cup (200 g) leftover risotto from Risotto with Roasted Butternut Squash (page 63)

1 tbsp (8 g) flour

1 large egg, beaten

¼ cup (30 g) bread crumbs, seasoned with ¼ tsp kosher salt

2 tbsp (30 ml) vegetable oil

Salad
1 tsp mayonnaise

¼ tsp dried Italian seasoning

1 pinch of salt

1 pinch of black pepper

1 tsp white wine vinegar

1 tbsp (15 ml) olive oil

2 cups (120 g) mixed greens

To make the risotto balls, divide the risotto into 4 equal parts and roll each into a ball. Lightly coat each ball in flour. Coat each ball in egg and let any excess drip off before rolling each in the bread crumbs. Place the balls on a plate and transfer the plate to the freezer for 10 minutes so they can set.

In a 10-inch (25-cm) nonstick skillet, heat the vegetable oil over medium heat. Before frying the balls, first test the oil by dropping a pinch of flour in the pan. If the oil bubbles around the flour right away, it's ready. Place the balls in the pan and fry them for 1 to 2 minutes, or until they're golden brown on the bottom. Turn them and continue frying them for 1 minute or so per side until they are golden and crispy all over. Transfer them to a plate lined with a paper towel.

To make the salad, whisk the mayonnaise, Italian seasoning, salt, pepper, vinegar and olive oil together in a medium-size bowl. Add the mixed greens and toss with the dressing. Serve with the risotto balls on the side.

BBQ Turkey Meatloaf
with Zucchini Fries

Ask ten different people for their best meatloaf recipe and you'll probably learn ten different ways to make it, because it seems meatloaf is a lot like snowflakes—no two are exactly the same. While this recipe calls for ground turkey, you can substitute ground beef to switch things up. Either works well with the no-cook BBQ glaze you brush on it as it bakes in the oven. The zucchini fries, which bake right alongside the meatloaf in the oven, are a fun twist on French fries.

Serves 1

Sauce

⅓ cup (80 ml) tomato sauce

1 tbsp (22 g) molasses

2 tsp (6 g) brown sugar

1 tbsp (15 ml) apple cider vinegar

¼ tsp kosher salt

¼ tsp red pepper flakes

¼ tsp dried oregano

¼ tsp garlic powder

¼ tsp onion powder

Meatloaf

¼ tsp kosher salt

¼ tsp black pepper

¼ tsp dried oregano

1½ tbsp (11 g) dried bread crumbs

1 egg, beaten

6 oz (170 g) ground turkey

Fries

½ cup (60 g) bread crumbs

½ tsp kosher salt

2 tbsp (16 g) all-purpose flour

1 egg

1 (6-oz [170-g]) zucchini, cut into ½" (1.3-cm)-thick sticks

Preheat the oven to 400°F (200°C). Line a baking sheet with foil and lightly coat it with cooking spray.

To make the sauce, combine the tomato sauce, molasses, sugar, vinegar, salt, red pepper flakes, oregano, garlic powder and onion powder in a small bowl. Set aside ¼ cup (68 g) of the sauce for serving, reserving the rest to glaze the meatloaf while it bakes.

To make the meatloaf, first combine the salt, pepper, oregano, bread crumbs and egg in a medium-size bowl. Add the ground turkey and use your hands to mix it with the egg and bread crumb mixture until it is just combined. Form the turkey into a loaf shape and place it on the prepared baking sheet, leaving space for the zucchini fries.

To make the fries, combine the bread crumbs and salt in a shallow bowl. Place the flour in a separate shallow bowl. Beat the egg in a third small bowl. Coat each of the zucchini fries in the flour, dip it in the egg and let the excess drip off, then roll it in the bread crumbs. Place all of the fries in a single layer on the baking sheet with the meatloaf.

Brush the meatloaf with a light coating of the BBQ sauce. Transfer the baking sheet to the oven and bake for 15 minutes. Brush the meatloaf with another coating of BBQ sauce and continue baking for another 10 minutes. Brush it again with the rest of the sauce and bake it for another 5 minutes. Let the meatloaf rest for a couple of minutes before slicing. To serve, spoon the reserved BBQ sauce over the top of the meatloaf and serve the zucchini fries on the side.

Molasses-Braised Short Ribs
with Pan-Seared Onions

Short ribs are a great choice for scaled-down recipes because they're typically sold in packages of four, and while they're small in size, they pack a big punch in flavor and richness. Here they are slow cooked for several hours in the oven with tomatoes, garlic, herbs and molasses, which gives the braising liquid a bit of body and adds a touch of sweetness to the ribs. The pan-seared onions topped with crispy bread crumbs are like deconstructed onion rings and go great with the rich and hearty ribs.

Serves 1

Short Ribs

2 tsp (10 ml) olive oil

2 (4-oz [115-g]) boneless beef short ribs

¼ cup (38 g) chopped yellow onion

2 tsp (6 g) minced garlic

½ cup (120 g) crushed tomatoes

1 tsp Worcestershire sauce

1 tbsp (22 g) molasses

1 bay leaf

½ tsp fresh thyme leaves

½ tsp kosher salt

½ tsp black pepper

1½ cups (355 ml) water

Onions

½ tbsp (4 g) bread crumbs

½ tsp kosher salt, divided

1 pinch of black pepper

1 pinch of dried oregano

¼ tsp olive oil

2 tsp (10 ml) vegetable oil

1 (6-oz [170-g]) yellow onion, cut into ¼" (6-mm) slices

1 tsp chopped fresh parsley, for garnish

Preheat the oven to 350°F (175°C).

To make the short ribs, heat the olive oil in a 3-quart (3-L) ovenproof saucepan over medium heat. Cook the short ribs in the oil for 5 minutes on each side, or until they are browned. Transfer the ribs to a clean plate. In the same pan, cook the onion and garlic for 1 minute. Add the tomatoes, Worcestershire sauce and molasses. Stir and bring to a simmer. Add the bay leaf, thyme, salt and pepper. Pour the water into the pan and stir to combine.

Adjust the heat and bring the liquid to a simmer before adding the ribs back to the pan. Place a lid on the pan slightly askew to allow steam to escape. Transfer the pan to the oven and cook the ribs for 2½ to 3 hours, or until the ribs easily shred. Remove the pan from the oven and leave it covered on the stove while you make the onions.

To make the onions, combine the bread crumbs, ¼ teaspoon of the salt, black pepper, oregano and olive oil in a small bowl. In a 10-inch (25-cm) nonstick skillet, toast the bread crumb mixture over medium heat until it is golden brown. Transfer the bread crumbs back to the small bowl and wipe out the pan with a paper towel.

In the same nonstick skillet, heat the vegetable oil over medium-high heat. Add the sliced onions and cook them for 3 to 4 minutes on each side, or until they take on a golden color and have softened. To serve, place the onions on a plate, season them with the remaining ¼ teaspoon of salt and sprinkle the bread crumbs and parsley over the top. Place the short ribs on the side with some of the braising liquid spooned over the top.

Three-Cheese Mushroom Manicotti

I believe if you're going to take the time to make a stuffed pasta dish, it's best to go all in and use the good stuff. In this recipe three manicotti are filled with ricotta cheese and earthy mushrooms, baked in a rich and creamy cheese sauce and topped with just a little more shredded cheese for good measure. Make this when you want to treat yourself.

Serves 1

Filling
2 tsp (10 ml) olive oil

6 oz (170 g) cremini mushrooms, finely chopped

2 tsp (6 g) minced garlic

¾ tsp kosher salt, divided

⅓ cup (41 g) ricotta cheese

2 tsp (2 g) chopped fresh parsley

½ cup (60 g) shredded mozzarella, divided

1 pinch of black pepper

Sauce
1 tbsp (14 g) unsalted butter

2 tsp (5 g) all-purpose flour

½ cup (120 ml) 2% milk

½ cup (90 g) shredded Parmesan, plus 1 tbsp (11 g), divided

4 manicotti, cooked according to package directions

Preheat the oven to 350°F (175°C).

To make the filling, heat the olive oil over medium heat in an 8½-inch (22-cm) skillet. Add the mushrooms, garlic and ½ teaspoon of the salt and stir. Cook the mixture for 8 to 10 minutes, or until the mushrooms have released their moisture. Transfer the mushrooms and garlic to a clean plate to cool.

In a small bowl, combine the ricotta, parsley, ¼ cup (30 g) of the mozzarella, the remaining ¼ teaspoon salt and the black pepper. Add the mushrooms and stir until combined.

To make the sauce, heat the butter over medium heat in the same pan that you cooked the mushrooms. Add the flour and stir until combined. Slowly add the milk, stirring continuously until smooth. Adjust the heat to maintain a gentle simmer (don't let it boil) and cook the sauce until it starts to thicken, about 5 minutes. Add ½ cup (90 g) of the Parmesan cheese and stir until it's melted and the sauce is smooth, 1 to 2 minutes.

Coat the bottom of a 20-ounce (590-ml) baking dish with 1 tablespoon (15 ml) of the cheese sauce. Divide the mushroom cheese filling into 4 equal parts. Stuff each manicotti with the filling and place them in the baking dish. Pour the cheese sauce over the top and sprinkle the remaining 1 tablespoon (11 g) Parmesan and remaining ¼ cup (30 g) mozzarella over the top. Cover the dish with foil and bake for 20 minutes. Remove the foil and bake for another 10 minutes. Let the manicotti stand for a few minutes before serving.

Tarragon Chicken *with* Roasted Parmesan Green Beans

Pan sauce is my favorite way to dress up a humble chicken breast, and it couldn't be easier to do. In the time it takes to roast the green beans, the chicken and sauce come together on the stove top with just some butter, white wine and herbs. The classic combination of tarragon, mustard and white wine makes this a dinner worth adding to your rotation.

Serves 1

4 oz (115 g) fresh green beans, stems removed

1 tsp olive oil

1 tbsp (14 g) unsalted butter

1 (6-oz [170-g]) boneless, skinless chicken breast, ½" (1.3 cm) thick, seasoned with kosher salt

1 tsp minced garlic

¼ cup (60 ml) dry white wine

½ tsp Dijon mustard

1 tsp chopped fresh tarragon

1 pinch of salt

1 pinch of black pepper

Juice of ½ lemon

1 tbsp (11 g) grated Parmesan cheese

Preheat the oven to 400°F (200°C).

Place the green beans in an even layer on a sheet pan. Drizzle the olive oil over the top of the green beans and lightly toss to coat them evenly in the oil. Roast the green beans for 20 minutes, or until they are crisp-tender.

In an 8½-inch (22-cm) skillet, melt the butter over medium heat. Place the chicken in the pan and cook it for 5 minutes on each side until it's browned. Transfer the chicken to a clean plate. In the same pan, add the garlic, wine, mustard and tarragon and stir to combine. Place the chicken back in the pan and cover it, cooking it in the sauce until it's cooked through, about 5 minutes.

Season the roasted green beans with salt and black pepper. Squeeze the lemon juice over the top of the green beans and top with the grated Parmesan cheese. Serve the chicken with the sauce spooned over the top and the green beans on the side.

Smothered Veggie *and* Bean Burrito

Just like a regular burrito but with roasted butternut squash instead of meat and finely chopped cauliflower instead of rice, this burrito is all rolled up with some pinto beans in a big tortilla and baked in a simple red chili sauce.

Serves 1

Squash
1 cup (135 g) diced butternut squash, cut into 1" (2.5-cm) pieces

1 tsp olive oil

1 pinch of kosher salt

1 pinch of black pepper

Cauliflower
1 tsp olive oil

1 cup (106 g) finely chopped cauliflower florets

¼ tsp kosher salt

1 pinch of black pepper

Beans
1 tbsp (14 g) unsalted butter

1 tsp all-purpose flour

¼ cup (60 ml) vegetable stock

1 cup (240 ml) tomato sauce

½ tsp ground cumin

½ tsp chili powder

2 tsp (2 g) chopped fresh cilantro, divided

⅓ cup (80 g) canned pinto beans, drained and rinsed

Burrito
1 (10" [25-cm]) tortilla

¼ cup (33 g) grated pepper Jack cheese

1 tbsp (8 g) sour cream, for garnish

Preheat the oven to 400°F (200°C).

To make the squash, spread it on a baking sheet and coat it evenly with the olive oil. Season the squash with the salt and pepper and roast it for 20 to 25 minutes, or until it's fork tender.

To make the cauliflower, heat the olive oil in an 8½-inch (22-cm) skillet over medium heat. Add the cauliflower, salt and black pepper. Cook the cauliflower for 8 to 10 minutes, stirring frequently, until it's softened and lightly golden in places. Transfer the cauliflower to a clean plate.

To make the beans, melt the butter over medium heat in the same skillet you used for the cauliflower. Add the flour and stir until it's combined with the butter. Slowly add the stock, stirring continuously until smooth. Bring the stock to a simmer and cook for 1 to 2 minutes, or until it starts to thicken. Add the tomato sauce, cumin, chili powder and 1 teaspoon of the cilantro. Stir and cook the sauce for 1 minute.

Ladle half of the sauce into a small bowl and set the bowl aside. Add the pinto beans to the reserved sauce in the pan and cook them long enough to just warm them through, 2 to 3 minutes. Mash the beans with a fork a few times to break them up.

To make the burrito, place the cauliflower just off the center of the tortilla, leaving space around the edge so you can fold in the ends. Top the cauliflower with the mashed pinto beans and roasted squash. Fold the tortilla over the top of the filling. Fold the open ends toward the filling and roll the burrito. Place the burrito seam-side down in an 8 x 8-inch (20 x 20-cm) baking dish and pour the reserved sauce over the top. Sprinkle the cheese over the top of the sauce. Cover the baking dish with foil and bake the burrito for 20 minutes. Uncover the dish and bake it for another 5 minutes. Garnish with the sour cream and the remaining 1 teaspoon chopped cilantro.

NOTES: Look for precut butternut squash in packages at the grocery store. The squash can be roasted ahead of time and kept in the refrigerator for a day until you are ready to use it.

You can also find pre-chopped cauliflower in packages. It's often called "cauliflower rice."

Kielbasa *with* Creamy Horseradish Pasta

In another place, you might serve slices of pan-seared kielbasa alongside whole cooked Brussels sprouts with a dollop of creamy horseradish on the side. Here we combine them all together in a pasta dish to mix things up. The shaved sprouts add a nice texture to the creamy sauce, which packs a bit of a spicy bite.

Serves 1

1 tsp olive oil

4 oz (115 g) kielbasa sausage, sliced ¼" (6 mm) thick

4 oz (115 g) fresh Brussels sprouts, sliced very thin

1 tbsp (15 ml) dry white wine

½ tsp kosher salt

1 tbsp (3 g) chopped fresh parsley, divided

¼ cup (60 ml) heavy cream

2 tsp (10 g) creamy prepared horseradish

2 oz (60 g) gemelli, cooked according to package directions

2 tbsp (30 ml) reserved pasta water

In an 8½-inch (22-cm) skillet, heat the olive oil over medium heat. Place the sausage slices in the pan and cook them for 2 minutes, or until they start to brown and release some of their fat. Turn the slices and cook them on the other side for 2 minutes. Transfer the sausage slices to a clean plate and set aside.

In the same pan, cook the sliced Brussels sprouts for 5 minutes, stirring frequently until they soften. Add the wine and simmer it, scraping any browned bits off the bottom of the pan, until it mostly evaporates, 30 to 60 seconds. Add the salt, half of the parsley, cream and horseradish. Stir and simmer until the sauce thickens, 1 to 2 minutes. Add the cooked pasta and sausage and stir to coat it in the sauce. Add up to 2 tablespoons (30 ml) of the reserved pasta water to thin the sauce, if needed. Garnish with the remaining parsley.

Little Meatballs *with* Parmesan Garlic Rice

When you cook meals for one, tasks that might otherwise be labor-intensive, like mixing and rolling meatballs, are easier to do. These little meatballs simmered in a savory tomato sauce and served over a simple Parmesan garlic rice are an easy way to get a comfort-food fix without a lot of work.

Serves 1

Meatballs
1 large egg

2 tbsp (15 g) bread crumbs

½ tsp dried oregano

¼ tsp red pepper flakes

½ tsp garlic powder

½ tsp kosher salt

½ tsp black pepper

4 oz (115 g) ground beef

1 tsp olive oil

Sauce
¼ cup (38 g) finely chopped yellow onion

1 tsp minced garlic

½ cup (60 g) finely chopped carrot

2 tsp (10 g) tomato paste

1 tsp all-purpose flour

2 tsp (10 ml) Worcestershire sauce

1 cup (235 ml) beef stock

½ tsp kosher salt

1 bay leaf

Leaves from 2 sprigs of fresh thyme

Rice
1 cup (235 ml) water

¼ cup (53 g) long-grain white rice

1 tsp minced garlic

1 tbsp (15 ml) heavy cream

½ tbsp (7 g) unsalted butter

1 tbsp (11 g) grated Parmesan cheese

1 tsp chopped fresh parsley

To make the meatballs, combine the egg, bread crumbs, oregano, red pepper flakes, garlic powder, salt and black pepper in a medium-size bowl. Add the beef and use your hands to mix it all together until it's just combined. Form meatballs with 1 tablespoon (15 g) of the beef for each ball.

Heat the olive oil in a 3½-quart (3-L) saucepan over medium heat. Add the meatballs and brown them on one side, about 2 minutes. Turn the meatballs and brown on the other side. Transfer the meatballs to a clean plate.

To make the sauce, add the onion to the pan and cook until they start to soften, 2 to 3 minutes. Add the garlic and carrot and cook for 1 to 2 minutes, or until the garlic is fragrant. Add the tomato paste and flour and stir to coat the vegetables. Pour in the Worcestershire sauce and stir, scraping up any browned bits off the bottom of the pan. Add the beef stock, salt, bay leaf and fresh thyme and stir to combine. Bring the stock to a simmer and place the meatballs in the sauce. Adjust the heat to low, cover the pan with the lid slightly askew and simmer the meatballs.

To make the rice, bring the water to a boil in a small saucepan. Add the rice and garlic and cover the pan. Reduce the heat to low. Cook until it's tender, about 20 minutes, stirring occasionally. Drain off any excess water. Stir in the cream and butter until melted, add the cheese and stir. Sprinkle with the parsley. Turn off the heat and cover to keep warm.

Uncover the meatballs and adjust the heat to medium to bring the sauce to a strong simmer. Cook it for another 5 minutes, or until the sauce has slightly thickened. Remove the bay leaf and serve the meatballs over the rice.

Braised Chicken *with* Smoked Cheddar Mac *and* Cheese

Growing up, macaroni and cheese was a much fought-over side dish at the dinner table. These days I make it a whole dinner by topping it with some tender braised chicken and a rich sauce made from the braising liquid the chicken is cooked low and slow in. This macaroni and cheese is an easy stove-top version for one (no sharing required!), but it's likely you'll have leftover chicken. It makes a great sandwich filling the next day!

Serves 1

Chicken
2 tsp (10 ml) olive oil

1 (1-lb [453-g]) bone-in, skin-on chicken breast, seasoned with salt and pepper

½ cup (76 g) finely diced onion

1 tbsp (10 g) minced garlic

½ cup (75 g) chopped red bell pepper, cut into 2" (5-cm) pieces

1 tbsp (9 g) canned diced mild or hot green chile

½ cup (121 g) crushed tomatoes

¼ tsp kosher salt

½ cup (120 ml) chicken stock

Juice of 1 lime

Smoked Cheddar Mac and Cheese
2 tbsp (30 ml) 2% milk, plus 2 tsp (10 ml) as needed, divided

¾ tsp cornstarch

Salt and black pepper

1½ tbsp (22 g) unsalted butter

½ cup (65 g) grated smoked cheddar cheese

¼ cup (33 g) grated fontina cheese

2 oz (60 g) penne, cooked according to package directions

1 tsp chopped fresh parsley

Preheat the oven to 350°F (175°C).

To make the chicken, in an oven-safe 3½-quart (3-L) saucepan, heat the olive oil over medium heat. Place the chicken skin-side down in the pan and cook it until the skin is golden brown, 5 to 10 minutes. Transfer the chicken to a plate. In the same pan, cook the onion, garlic and bell pepper for 2 to 3 minutes, or until the vegetables start to soften. Add the green chile, crushed tomatoes, salt, chicken stock and lime juice. Stir and adjust the heat to bring the liquid to a boil. Place the chicken back in the pan, cover with the lid slightly askew and transfer the pan to the oven. Cook the chicken for 30 to 40 minutes, or until the internal temperature is 165°F (74°C).

Remove the pan from the oven. Transfer the chicken to a cutting board. Strain the liquid into a bowl using a fine-mesh strainer. Discard the solids and pour the strained liquid back into the saucepan. Over high heat, bring the liquid to a boil and reduce it for 15 to 20 minutes. While the liquid reduces, shred the chicken and discard the skin and bones. Once the sauce is reduced and thickened, add the shredded chicken and adjust the heat to medium-low.

To make the macaroni and cheese, in a small bowl, whisk 2 tablespoons (30 ml) of the milk with the cornstarch, then season with salt and pepper. In a small saucepan, melt the butter. Add the milk and cornstarch mixture and whisk it with the butter for 1 minute, or until it starts to thicken. Add the cheeses and stir continuously until it's smooth and creamy, 1 to 2 minutes. Add up to 2 teaspoons (10 ml) of the remaining milk if the cheese sauce is too thick. Serve the pasta and shredded chicken topped with the sauce. Garnish with the chopped parsley.

30-Minute Single-Serving Dinners

As much as I love kitchen cooking projects—recipes best suited for weekends when there's more time, patience and willingness to enjoy the process of cooking as much as the actual meal itself—there are times when that love is sucked right out the window by a busy weekday. For those days, when time is short and patience is shorter, a 30-minute dinner can save the day (or at the very least save us from ordering takeout).

On those nights when drive-throughs and delivery are so tempting, I tend to satisfy my cravings with easy make-at-home versions of those things I might have ordered in—like Crispy Fish Tacos with Radish–Citrus Slaw (page 104), which is light on oil but big on fresh flavor, or Ginger Beef Lo Mein (page 92), which is ready to go in the time it would take to have it delivered from my neighborhood takeout place. There are also a few reinvented pasta recipes in this chapter and a few familiar favorites. All of them together make a great playbook for weeknight cooking.

Pappardelle *with* Roasted Red Pepper Pesto *and* Sautéed Fennel

Fresh fennel has a licorice flavor, but when it's caramelized in a hot pan, its natural sweetness emerges. Use the wispy fronds attached to the fennel stems in both the red pepper pesto and as a garnish for this easy pasta dinner.

Serves 1

Pesto

½ cup (115 g) roughly chopped roasted red peppers

¼ cup (31 g) chopped hazelnuts

1 large clove garlic, roughly chopped

¼ cup (45 g) shredded Asiago cheese, plus 1 tbsp (11 g) for garnish

¼ cup (10 g) chopped fennel fronds

1 tsp kosher salt

2 tbsp (30 g) olive oil

2 oz (60 g) pappardelle

Fennel

1 tsp olive oil

1 tbsp (14 g) butter

1 (8-oz [227-g]) fennel bulb, stems removed, quartered and sliced

2 tbsp (30 ml) water

½ tsp kosher salt

¼ tsp black pepper

To make the pesto, pulse the red pepper, hazelnuts, garlic, cheese, fennel fronds and salt in a small food processor or blender until a paste forms. Slowly add the olive oil, with the food processor or blender running, until it's fully incorporated.

Boil the pasta according to package directions.

While the pasta cooks, start the fennel by heating the olive oil and butter in an 8½-inch (22-cm) skillet. Add the fennel and cook until it starts to caramelize on both sides, stirring occasionally, about 5 minutes. Add the water to the pan and cover it with a lid. Cook the fennel for 5 minutes, or until it's fork tender. Reduce the heat to low and stir the fennel occasionally until about a minute or so before the pasta is ready. Add all of the red pepper pesto to the pan with the fennel. Adjust the heat to medium and stir to coat the fennel in the sauce. Transfer the cooked pasta to the skillet, using tongs to toss it with the sauce and fennel. Garnish with the remaining 1 tablespoon (11 g) shredded Asiago cheese and season with salt and pepper.

Chicken Gyro Salad

A salad as a main dish needs to be filling, and making a dish that would normally be a pita stuffed with chicken, tomatoes, onion and creamy cool dressing into a salad accomplishes just that. The recipe makes enough for two servings, so keep the leftover components separate and toss them together the next day for lunch.

Serves 2

Marinade

2 tsp (10 ml) olive oil, divided

½ tsp dried oregano

½ tsp ground cumin

¼ tsp kosher salt

1 (8-oz [227-g]) boneless, skinless chicken breast

Dressing

½ cup (100 g) plain Greek yogurt

Juice of ½ lemon

2 tsp (6 g) minced garlic

2 tsp (2 g) chopped fresh dill

Salt, to taste

1 tsp olive oil

Salad

4 cups (145 g) chopped green leaf lettuce

1 cup (150 g) grape or cherry tomatoes, halved

¼ small red onion, thinly sliced

1 (7-oz [198-g]) cucumber, sliced ¼" (6 mm) thick

1 tbsp (3 g) chopped fresh parsley

¼ cup (38 g) crumbled feta cheese

2 pita, quartered

To make the marinade, combine 1 teaspoon of the olive oil, oregano, cumin and salt in a shallow bowl. Place the chicken in the marinade and turn it a few times to coat it evenly. Set the bowl aside while you make the dressing.

To make the dressing, mix the yogurt, lemon juice, garlic, dill, salt and olive oil in a small bowl until combined. Place the bowl in the refrigerator to chill while you cook the chicken.

Prepare the chicken by heating the remaining 1 teaspoon of olive oil over medium heat. Place the chicken in the pan and brown it on both sides for 4 to 5 minutes, or until the chicken is cooked through. Remove the chicken from the pan and let it rest on a cutting board for a few minutes before cutting it into 1-inch (2.5-cm) cubes.

To make the salad, place the lettuce in a large bowl. Top it with the tomatoes, onion, cucumber and chicken. Drizzle the dressing over the top and sprinkle the parsley and cheese over the dressing. Serve with the pita bread.

Sausage-Stuffed Mushroom Caps

These simple stuffed mushrooms are like pizza without the crust. Look for portobello mushroom caps, usually sold in packages of two, that have a lip around the edge to help hold the filling. I like to precook them in a skillet to help release moisture so they don't come out of the oven soggy. Serve them with the Italian salad on the side for a veggie-packed dinner.

Serves 1

Mushrooms
2 (3-oz [85-g]) portobello mushroom caps, stems and gills removed

1 tsp olive oil

1 tsp kosher salt, divided

1 (3-oz [85-g]) Italian sausage link, casing removed

¼ cup (38 g) finely diced onion

2 tsp (6 g) minced garlic

1 tbsp (15 ml) balsamic vinegar

¼ cup (60 g) crushed tomatoes

½ tsp dried Italian seasoning

½ cup (60 g) shredded mozzarella

Salad
¼ tsp balsamic vinegar

1 pinch of kosher salt

1 pinch of black pepper

¾ tsp olive oil

2 cups (120 g) mixed greens

1 tbsp (11 g) grated Parmesan cheese, for garnish

1 tsp chopped fresh parsley, for garnish

Preheat the oven to 400°F (200°C). Line a baking sheet with foil.

To make the mushrooms, first rub each mushroom with the olive oil. Season each mushroom with ¼ teaspoon of salt each. Heat an 8½-inch (22-cm) skillet over medium heat. Place 1 mushroom cap in the pan and cook it on one side for 2 to 3 minutes, or until it starts to release some moisture. Turn it over and cook it on the other side for 2 to 3 minutes. Transfer it to the baking sheet and repeat the same process for the other mushroom cap. As the mushrooms rest on the sheet pan, they will continue releasing moisture. Use a paper towel to blot the moisture before you stuff them.

In the same skillet, add the sausage and cook until browned, breaking it up while it cooks, about 5 minutes. Add the onion, garlic and balsamic vinegar. As the vinegar simmers scrape up any browned bits off the bottom of the pan. Add the tomatoes, the remaining ½ teaspoon salt and the Italian seasoning. Stir and simmer the sauce for 5 minutes. Spoon the filling into the mushrooms and top each with half the mozzarella cheese. Transfer the baking sheet to the oven and bake the mushrooms for 10 to 15 minutes, or until the mushrooms are tender.

To make the salad, combine the vinegar, salt, pepper and olive oil in a medium-size bowl. Place the greens in the bowl and gently toss to coat them evenly with the dressing. Transfer the salad to a plate. Place the baked mushrooms on the plate with the salad and garnish both with the Parmesan and parsley.

BLT Chicken Pasta

If you combined a BLT sandwich with chicken pasta, this is what you'd get. Fresh tomatoes, spinach, smoky bacon and tender pasta combined with chicken and a simple mayo sauce takes the flavors of a lunchtime staple and turns them into dinner.

Serves 1

1 tbsp (14 g) mayonnaise

1 tbsp (8 g) sour cream

1 tsp lemon zest

Juice of 1 lemon, divided

1 slice thick-cut bacon, cut into 2" (5-cm) pieces

1 (4-oz [115-g]) boneless, skinless chicken breast, sliced in half horizontally into 2 equal-size pieces

3 oz (85 g) cherry tomatoes, halved

2 cups (60 g) roughly chopped fresh spinach

½ tsp kosher salt

2 oz (60 g) penne, cooked according to package directions

2 tsp (2 g) chopped fresh parsley, for garnish

In a small-size bowl, combine the mayonnaise, sour cream, zest and juice from ½ lemon. Set the bowl aside.

In an 8½-inch (22-cm) skillet, cook the bacon over medium heat until it's crispy, 2 to 3 minutes. Transfer the bacon to a plate lined with a paper towel and leave the fat in the pan. In the same pan, cook the chicken breast in the bacon fat for 5 minutes. Turn it and cook it on the other side for 5 minutes, or until it's cooked through. Transfer the chicken to a cutting board and slice it into ¼-inch (6-mm) pieces.

In the same pan, cook the tomatoes with the remaining lemon juice for 3 to 4 minutes, or until the tomatoes start to break down. Add the spinach and cook it for 2 minutes, or until it wilts. Add the salt and stir. Add the cooked pasta and the chicken to the pan. Stir to combine and turn off the heat. Add the mayonnaise sauce and stir to coat the pasta. Roughly chop the bacon and sprinkle it over the pasta. Garnish with the parsley and serve.

Ginger Beef Lo Mein

If you've ever wondered how your takeout order arrives so fast, it's either because the dishes you ordered were already made before you called or because they're so simple to make that they take hardly any time. Both are good reasons to toss the menus and give this takeout-inspired dinner a try.

Serves 1

2 tbsp (30 ml) soy sauce

1 tbsp (15 ml) rice wine vinegar

1 tbsp (12 g) minced ginger

1 tsp chopped garlic

1 tsp sesame oil

2 tsp (8 g) brown sugar

1 tsp cornstarch

2 tsp (10 ml) vegetable oil

3 oz (85 g) beef sirloin, thinly sliced and seasoned with salt

½ cup (33 g) sliced baby bella mushrooms

1 cup (91 g) roughly chopped broccoli florets

1 cup (115 g) thinly sliced red onion

½ cup (45 g) chopped green cabbage

2 oz (60 g) dry lo mein noodles, cooked according to package directions

1 scallion, sliced, for garnish

Combine the soy sauce, vinegar, ginger, garlic, oil and brown sugar in a small bowl. Add the cornstarch and whisk until smooth.

In a 10-inch (25-cm) skillet, heat the oil over medium heat. Place the sliced beef in an even layer in the pan. Brown the beef for 2 to 3 minutes on each side. Transfer the beef to a plate and set it aside.

Add the mushrooms to the pan and cook them until they are browned on both sides, 2 to 3 minutes. Add the broccoli florets to the pan and cook them with the mushrooms for 5 minutes, stirring frequently. Add the onion, cabbage and all of the sauce to the pan. Bring the sauce to a simmer and add the beef back to the pan, stirring to combine. Add the cooked noodles and stir to coat the noodles in the sauce. Top with the sliced scallion and serve.

Baja Turkey Burger

Inspired by the tacos you might find at a beach-adjacent restaurant, this turkey burger is topped with crisp coleslaw and a creamy avocado spread.

Serves 1

1 tbsp (13 g) minced red onion

1 tsp chopped fresh cilantro

Juice of 1 lime, divided

1 tbsp (11 g) finely diced jalapeño

¼ cup (22 g) finely chopped green cabbage

2 oz (60 g) cherry or grape tomatoes, quartered

½ tsp kosher salt, divided

¼ cup (38 g) diced avocado

2 tsp (5 g) sour cream

1 tsp olive oil

4 oz (115 g) ground turkey, formed into a ¼" (6-mm)-thick patty and seasoned with salt and pepper

1 hamburger bun

In a small-size bowl, combine the red onion, cilantro, half of the lime juice, jalapeño, cabbage and tomatoes. Add ¼ teaspoon of the salt, stir and set the bowl aside.

In a separate small-size bowl, mash the avocado with a fork. Add the sour cream, the remaining lime juice and the remaining ¼ teaspoon salt and stir to combine. Set the bowl aside.

In an 8½-inch (22-cm) nonstick skillet, heat the olive oil over medium heat. Cook the turkey patty for 4 to 5 minutes on one side until it's browned. Turn the burger and cook it on the other side for 4 to 5 minutes, or until it is cooked through. To serve, place the cabbage slaw on the bottom bun and top with the burger, then the avocado and the top bun slice.

NOTE: A head of cabbage will leave you with way more cabbage than you need, so look for bags of pre-chopped cabbage in the produce department.

Roasted Pepper Baked Penne *with* Peas *and* Ham

Spanish-inspired flavors meet pasta. This is a great way to switch up boring pasta and tomato sauce night by tossing familiar ingredients like ham and peas with pasta and a roasted red pepper sauce.

Serves 1

2 tsp (10 ml) olive oil

¼ cup (34 g) diced ham

¼ cup (38 g) finely chopped onion

1 tsp minced garlic

½ cup (120 ml) pureed roasted red peppers

½ tsp paprika

½ tsp kosher salt

1 pinch of black pepper

¼ cup (38 g) frozen green peas

2 tbsp (30 ml) heavy cream

3 oz (85 g) orecchiette, cooked according to package directions

2 tbsp (30 ml) reserved pasta water

⅓ cup (60 g) grated Manchengo cheese

1 tsp chopped fresh parsley

In an 8½-inch (22-cm) skillet, heat the olive oil over medium heat. Add the ham and cook it in the oil for 2 to 3 minutes. Add the onion and garlic and cook them just until the garlic is fragrant, about 1 minute. Add the pepper puree, paprika, salt and pepper. Stir and simmer the sauce for 5 minutes. Add the peas and cook them in the sauce, stirring frequently, until they are warmed through, 2 to 3 minutes.

Add the cream and stir to combine. Add the cooked pasta and stir to coat it in the sauce. If needed, add up to 2 tablespoons (30 ml) of the reserved pasta water to the sauce to thin it. Serve the pasta with the cheese and parsley sprinkled on top.

NOTE: A 12-ounce (340-g) jar of roasted red peppers will yield ½ cup (120 ml) pureed peppers. Drain and rinse the peppers before pureeing in a blender.

Summer Berry Chicken Salad

During the summer when I cook chicken for dinner, I like to make a little extra to keep in the refrigerator for chicken salad sandwiches the next day. This version has a little bit of summer in each bite with some fresh blueberries and strawberries. Served on buttery croissants, it's a no-cook dinner for those nights when you don't want to turn on the stove.

Serves 2

¼ cup (55 g) mayonnaise

1 tsp chopped fresh basil

1 tsp lemon zest

½ tsp lemon juice

1 pinch of kosher salt

2 tbsp (19 g) chopped red onion

1 tbsp (15 g) slivered almonds

2 cups (280 g) diced cooked chicken breast

¼ cup (42 g) sliced strawberries

¼ cup (35 g) blueberries

2 leaves of green leaf lettuce

2 large croissants, sliced in half

In a large bowl, combine the mayonnaise, basil, lemon zest, lemon juice and salt. Add the red onion, almonds, chicken, strawberries and blueberries and stir until combined.

Place a lettuce leaf on one half of each croissant. Divide the salad between each croissant and serve.

Poblano Black Bean Rice
and Chicken Bowl

Like a burrito without the tortilla, this dish features rice loaded with spices, fresh poblano pepper, black beans and a simple pan-cooked chicken breast. Serve it as is or dress it up with your favorite burrito toppings like sour cream, guacamole and salsa.

Serves 1

Rice
1 tsp olive oil

½ cup (85 g) finely chopped poblano pepper

¼ cup (38 g) chopped red onion

¼ tsp kosher salt

1 tsp chili powder

1 cup (235 ml) chicken stock

¼ cup (53 g) long-grain white rice

½ cup (120 g) drained and rinsed canned black beans

Juice of 1 lime

1 tsp chopped fresh cilantro

Chicken
1 (4-oz [115-g]) boneless, skinless chicken breast, ½" (1.3 cm) thick

1 tsp chili powder

½ tsp kosher salt

1 tsp olive oil

To make the rice, heat the olive oil over medium heat in a 2-quart (2-L) saucepan. Add the pepper, onion and salt. Cook the vegetables for 2 to 3 minutes, or until they start to soften. Add the chili powder and chicken stock. Adjust the heat to bring the stock to a boil, add the rice and stir to combine. Adjust the heat to maintain a strong simmer and cook the rice, stirring occasionally, for 15 minutes. Add the black beans, lime juice and cilantro. Cook the rice for 5 minutes, or until it's tender and the liquid is absorbed.

While the rice cooks, make the chicken. First, season the chicken on both sides with the chili powder and salt. In an 8½-inch (22-cm) skillet, heat the olive oil over medium heat. Place the chicken in the pan and cook it for 4 to 5 minutes on the first side. Turn it and cook the other side for 5 minutes, or until the internal temperature is 165°F (74°C). Transfer the chicken to a cutting board and cover it loosely with foil until the rice is finished cooking.

To serve, slice the chicken into ¼-inch (6-mm) slices and place it on top of the rice.

Turkey Lettuce Wraps *with* Cucumber Salad

Like other takeout-inspired dishes, these lettuce wraps made with turkey and a simple sauce go from pan to plate in a short amount of time. The cool and crisp cucumber salad is a nice contrast to the hot and savory filling.

Serves 1

Cucumber Salad

1 tbsp (15 ml) rice wine vinegar

½ tsp honey

1 tsp chopped fresh parsley

½ cup (67 g) diced cucumber

Sauce

2 tbsp (30 ml) soy sauce

2 tbsp (30 ml) rice wine vinegar

Juice of ½ lime

1 tsp sesame oil

1 tbsp (13 g) brown sugar

2 tsp (10 g) grated ginger

½ tsp red pepper flakes

1 tsp cornstarch

Turkey

2 tsp (10 ml) vegetable oil

5 oz (142 g) ground turkey

2 tsp (6 g) minced garlic

⅓ cup (50 g) diced red bell pepper

Green leaf lettuce, for wraps

To make the cucumber salad, combine the vinegar, honey and parsley in a small bowl. Toss the cucumber in the bowl with the dressing and place the bowl in the refrigerator to chill.

To make the sauce, whisk the soy sauce, vinegar, lime juice, oil, brown sugar, ginger, red pepper flakes and cornstarch in a small bowl until combined.

To make the turkey, heat the oil in an 8½-inch (22-cm) skillet over medium heat. Add the turkey, garlic and bell pepper. Cook, stirring frequently and breaking up the turkey as it cooks, until the turkey is cooked through, about 5 minutes. Add the sauce to the pan and stir. Simmer the sauce until it's thickened, 3 to 4 minutes. To serve, wrap the salad and turkey in lettuce leaves.

Crispy Fish Tacos *with* Radish–Citrus Slaw

Fish tacos are one of those favorite menu items I avoided making at home for a long time due to my aversion to deep frying. What do you do with all that leftover oil? Turns out you don't need it to get crispy breaded fish. A little oil in a nonstick skillet is just enough to make great fish tacos at home.

Serves 1

Slaw
½ cup (75 g) finely diced radishes

¼ cup (22 g) finely chopped green cabbage (see note)

1 tsp lemon juice

1 tbsp (14 g) mayonnaise

2 tsp (2 g) chopped fresh parsley, divided

¼ tsp kosher salt

Fish
⅓ cup (41 g) all-purpose flour

½ tsp ground cumin

½ tsp chili powder

¼ tsp paprika

1 tsp kosher salt

¼ tsp pepper

¼ tsp garlic powder

¼ cup (60 ml) water

4 oz (115 g) tilapia fillet, sliced into 1" (2.5-cm) slices

2 tbsp (30 ml) vegetable oil, divided

For Serving
3 small (5" [13-cm]) flour tortillas, charred lightly in a dry pan

Lime wedges, for serving

To make the slaw, combine the radishes, cabbage, lemon juice, mayonnaise, 1 teaspoon of the parsley and the salt in a medium-size bowl. Place the bowl in the refrigerator to keep the slaw cold while you prepare the fish.

To make the batter for the fish, whisk the flour, cumin, chili powder, paprika, salt, pepper and garlic powder in a medium-size bowl. Add the water and stir until the batter is smooth. Place the sliced fish in the bowl and stir to coat it evenly in the batter.

In a 10-inch (25-cm) nonstick skillet, heat 1 tablespoon (15 ml) of the oil over medium-high heat. Drop a pinch of flour in the pan. If the oil bubbles up quickly, it's ready. Place half of the battered fish slices in the pan. Fry them on each side until the batter is cooked and golden brown, approximately 2 to 3 minutes per side. Transfer the cooked fish to a plate lined with a paper towel. Add the remaining 1 tablespoon (15 ml) oil to the pan and repeat the process with the second batch of battered fish. Transfer the cooked fish to the plate lined with a paper towel.

To serve, divide the radish slaw between the tortillas. Top with the fish, squeeze fresh lime juice over the top and sprinkle the remaining 1 teaspoon parsley to garnish.

NOTE: A whole head of cabbage will yield way more cabbage than you need, so look for pre-chopped green cabbage in the produce department near the bagged lettuce.

Mediterranean-Inspired Chicken Pasta

This chicken pasta borrows flavors from the Mediterranean and is a snap to make. Using marinated sun-dried tomatoes and artichokes adds lots of flavor without a long ingredient list or too much time spent doing prep work. The recipe calls for penne, but any short pasta (like gemelli or ziti) will work well, too.

Serves 1

2 tsp (10 ml) olive oil

4 oz (115 g) boneless, skinless chicken breast, seasoned with kosher salt

¼ cup (28 g) chopped marinated sun-dried tomatoes

¼ cup (28 g) chopped marinated artichoke hearts

1 tsp minced garlic

2 oz (60 g) penne, cooked according to package directions

Juice of 1 lemon

¼ cup (45 g) grated Parmesan cheese

1 tsp chopped fresh parsley, for garnish

Heat the olive oil in an 8½-inch (22-cm) skillet over medium heat. Place the chicken in the skillet and cook it for 5 to 7 minutes per side, until it's cooked through. Transfer the chicken to a clean plate. In the same pan, combine the tomatoes, artichoke hearts and garlic and cook them for 2 to 3 minutes, or until they are warmed through. Slice the chicken breast into bite-size pieces and add it back to the pan.

Add the cooked pasta to the pan and stir to combine it with the rest of the ingredients. Add the lemon juice and stir. Serve with the cheese and parsley sprinkled over the top.

Italian-Style Tostadas

Italian tostadas are just like Mexican tostadas except instead of pinto beans you use cannellini beans to make quick and easy refried beans. They're topped with mozzarella and Parmesan cheese and garnished with fresh basil and Kalamata olives for an Italian twist.

Serves 1

2 tsp (10 ml) vegetable oil

3 (5" [13-cm]) corn tortillas

1 (3.5-oz [100-g]) mild Italian sausage

1 cup (240 g) cannellini beans

½ tsp balsamic vinegar

¼ tsp garlic powder

¼ tsp Italian seasoning

¼ tsp kosher salt

1 pinch of black pepper

2 tbsp (30 ml) water

⅓ cup (50 g) grated mozzarella cheese

¼ cup (40 g) grated Parmesan cheese

1 tbsp (3 g) sliced basil, for garnish

¼ cup (30 g) pitted and sliced Kalamata olives, for garnish

In a 10-inch (25-cm) nonstick skillet, heat the oil over medium-high heat until it's hot, but not smoking. Place a tortilla in the pan and fry it for 1 minute on each side, or until it's crispy. Transfer the tortilla to a plate lined with a paper towel. Repeat this process with the other two tortillas. Lower the heat on the pan to medium.

In the same pan, cook the sausage for 4 to 5 minutes or until it's cooked through, breaking it apart as it cooks. Transfer the sausage to a clean plate and set it aside.

In the same pan, cook the cannellini for 1 to 2 minutes, or until they're warmed through. Add the balsamic, garlic powder, Italian seasoning, salt and pepper and stir to coat the beans. Add the water to the pan. Using a potato masher or fork, mash the beans until they are broken down and mostly smooth. If the beans are too dry, add another tablespoon (15 ml) of water. Turn the heat off the pan.

Preheat the broiler with the oven rack about 6 inches (15 cm) below the heating element.

Place the tortillas in a single layer on a baking sheet. Top each tostada with one-third of the mashed beans, spreading them into an even layer. Top each tostada with the sausage, mozzarella and Parmesan cheese. Place the sheet pan under the broiler in the oven and broil the tostadas for 2 to 3 minutes or until the cheese is melted. Garnish the tostadas with the basil and olives.

Parmesan-Crusted Chicken Cutlet
with Avocado Tomato Salad

Chicken cutlets are just regular boneless, skinless chicken breasts sliced thin. You can buy cutlets at the store or just slice your own using the chicken breasts you might already have on hand. This crispy chicken crusted with Parmesan cheese and bread crumbs is great on a warm evening with the fresh avocado tomato salad on the side.

Serves 1

Salad

1 tsp lemon juice

1 tbsp (15 ml) olive oil

2 pinches of kosher salt, divided

1 cup (30 g) roughly chopped spinach

½ cup (75 g) diced avocado

2 oz (60 g) cherry or grape tomatoes, halved

1 tbsp (3 g) thinly sliced basil leaves

Chicken

1 tbsp (8 g) fine bread crumbs

1 tbsp (11 g) grated Parmesan cheese

¼ tsp dried oregano

¼ tsp kosher salt

2 pinches of black pepper

1 (6-oz [170-g]) chicken cutlet, ¼" (6 mm) thick

2 tsp (10 ml) olive oil

To make the salad, combine the lemon juice, oil and 1 pinch of the salt in a medium-size bowl. Add the spinach and toss it in the dressing until it is evenly coated. Pile the spinach on a serving plate and top with the diced avocado, tomatoes and basil leaves. Sprinkle the remaining 1 pinch salt over the top of the salad.

To make the chicken, combine the bread crumbs, cheese, oregano, salt and pepper in a shallow bowl. Coat the chicken in the bread crumbs. In an 8½-inch (22-cm) nonstick skillet, heat the olive oil over medium heat. Place the chicken in the skillet and cook it for 4 to 5 minutes on the first side, or until a golden crust forms. Turn it and cook it on the other side for 4 to 5 minutes, or until the chicken is cooked through. Serve the chicken with the salad on the side.

Shrimp *and* Veggies *in* Citrus Sauce

This bright and citrusy shrimp dish is a far cry from what you might order for takeout or pick up in the frozen section of the grocery store, and in the time it takes to order takeout, you can make it yourself. It's a fast-moving recipe starting with broccoli and bell pepper cooked together in some lemon juice. Add the shrimp and a sauce made with fresh orange juice and dinner is ready to go in about twenty minutes.

Serves 1

¼ cup (60 ml) fresh orange juice

1 tsp orange zest

2 tsp (10 ml) honey

½ tsp ginger paste

1 tsp minced garlic

1 tsp soy sauce

1 tsp sesame oil

½ tsp cornstarch

2 tsp (10 ml) vegetable oil

1 cup (91 g) broccoli florets

¼ cup (45 g) diced red bell pepper, cut into ½" (1.3-cm) pieces

¼ cup (38 g) finely diced red onion

¼ tsp kosher salt

Juice of 1 lemon

4 oz (115 g) raw shrimp, 51/60 count size, peeled and deveined

1 cup (161 g) cooked white rice

In a small-size bowl, whisk the orange juice, zest, honey, ginger, garlic, soy sauce, sesame oil and cornstarch until combined. Set the bowl aside.

In an 8½-inch (22-cm) skillet, heat the oil over medium-high heat. Place the broccoli in the pan and cook it for 1 to 2 minutes, or until it starts to turn brown in places. Adjust the heat to medium and add the bell pepper, red onion and salt and stir to combine. Add the lemon juice, stir and cover the pan with a lid. Cook the vegetables for 3 to 4 minutes, or until they start to soften.

Uncover the pan and add the shrimp and sauce. Stir to combine and cover the pan with a lid for 2 minutes, adjusting the heat to maintain a strong simmer. Uncover the pan and cook for another 3 to 4 minutes, stirring, or until the shrimp are opaque and cooked through. Serve with the cooked rice.

Steak *and* Peppers *with* Summer Herb Orzo

I can't help but think of this recipe as the Italian version of one of my Mexican restaurant favorites: steak fajitas. Instead of spicy seasonings, the steak and peppers of this recipe are flavored with Italian herbs and lots of fresh garlic, and instead of wrapping it all up in tortillas, you serve the tender beef and peppers with a generous helping of orzo pasta made with fresh herbs, bright lemon and a handful of Parmesan cheese.

Serves 1

Steak and Peppers

2 tsp (10 ml) olive oil, divided

½ tsp balsamic vinegar

1 pinch of kosher salt

1 pinch of black pepper

¼ tsp dried Italian seasoning

1 large clove garlic, roughly chopped

1 (6-oz [170-g]) sirloin steak

½ large red bell pepper, sliced ⅛" (3 mm) thick

6 slices red onion, sliced ⅛" (3 mm) thick

Juice from 1 lemon, divided

Orzo

2 cups (470 ml) water

½ cup (60 g) orzo

1 tsp chopped fresh basil

1 tsp chopped fresh parsley

½ tsp kosher salt

¼ cup (45 g) grated Parmesan cheese

To make the steak and peppers, combine 1 teaspoon of the olive oil, the balsamic vinegar, salt, pepper, Italian seasoning and garlic in a resealable bag. Place the steak in the bag, seal it and move it around to coat it in the marinade. Place it in the refrigerator for 30 minutes to 1 hour.

To make the orzo, bring the water to a boil in a 2-quart (2-L) saucepan. Add the orzo and cook it for 10 minutes, or until it's tender.

While the orzo is cooking, heat the remaining 1 teaspoon olive oil over medium heat in an 8½-inch (22-cm) skillet. Remove the steak from the marinade and pat it dry on both sides with a paper towel. Place the steak in the pan and cook it for 4 to 5 minutes on each side, or until it's browned. Transfer the steak to a cutting board.

Place the peppers and onion in the same pan and squeeze juice from half the lemon into the pan. Scrape up the browned bits off the bottom of the pan and cook the peppers and onions for 5 minutes, or until they start to soften. Slice the steak against the grain into ¼-inch (6-mm) slices. Add the sliced steak to the pan with the peppers. Adjust the heat to low while you finish making the orzo.

Drain the orzo and return it back to the same pan. Adjust the heat to low. Add the remaining lemon juice, basil, parsley, salt and cheese. Stir until combined. Transfer the orzo onto a plate and serve with the steak and peppers.

Artichoke Pasta *with* Chicken

Having a well-stocked kitchen means you can pull simple dinners together without much thought. This recipe uses ingredients I like to always have on hand, like frozen vegetables, chicken stock, fresh lemon, pasta and cheese. They add a lot of flavor to what might otherwise be a package of boring ground chicken, and all of it comes together in less than thirty minutes.

Serves 1

1 tbsp (15 ml) olive oil

4 oz (115 g) ground chicken

¼ tsp kosher salt

2 tsp (6 g) minced garlic

Juice of 1 lemon, divided

1 cup (240 g) frozen artichoke hearts

2 oz (60 g) frozen chopped spinach

¼ cup (60 ml) chicken stock

2 oz (60 g) gemelli pasta, cooked according to package directions

2 tbsp (22 g) grated Parmesan cheese

1 tsp chopped fresh parsley, for garnish

In an 8½-inch (22-cm) skillet, heat the olive oil over medium heat. Add the chicken and break it up with a spatula as it cooks. Once it's no longer pink, 3 to 4 minutes, add the salt, garlic and juice from half of the lemon. As the lemon juice bubbles in the pan, scrape up any browned bits on the bottom of the pan. Add the artichoke hearts, spinach and chicken stock. Cover the pan and simmer for 10 minutes, or until the artichokes and spinach are warmed through.

Add the cooked pasta and stir. Add the remaining lemon juice and cook the pasta for 1 minute. To serve, top the pasta with the grated cheese and garnish with the fresh parsley.

Simple One-Pan, One-Pot and Sheet-Pan Dinners

Dinner that comes together in just one skillet, on one sheet pan or in one pot is a dinner that's not only easier to clean up, but it's also easier (and sometimes faster!) to make.

But it's not always as simple as throwing a bunch of ingredients into a pot and calling it good. There's a science to a well-executed one-pot meal, and it's in knowing how long individual ingredients need to cook so that all of it comes out of the oven or off the stove at the right level of doneness.

We also have to let go of some standing cooking rules. For example, pasta doesn't always have to cook on its own in a separate pot, beef stroganoff can be served low-key straight from the skillet with just some toast on the side, and eggs—whether they're cooked in a spicy sauce or baked with potatoes and cheese—don't have to stay in the for-breakfast-only cooking column.

These recipes strive to be low-maintenance and quick, guide you along the path of what should go in before what and certainly break some rules. But the risks are worth it for a dinner that doesn't leave you with a sink full of dishes.

Skillet Zucchini Parmesan

I think of this as a deconstructed zucchini Parmesan—it tastes just like regular zucchini Parmesan without the hassle of breading and pan-frying the zucchini slices. All the best parts are here—fresh zucchini, crispy bread crumbs and quick tomato sauce—just rearranged for a weeknight dinner.

Serves 1

3 tsp (15 ml) olive oil, divided

8 oz (225 g) zucchini, cut into 3" (7.5-cm)-long wedges

2 tsp (6 g) chopped garlic

½ tsp dried Italian seasoning

½ tsp kosher salt

1 cup (242 g) crushed tomatoes

½ cup (120 ml) water

2 oz (60 g) penne pasta

2 tsp (5 g) bread crumbs

½ tsp kosher salt

1 tbsp (11 g) shredded Parmesan cheese

¼ cup (30 g) shredded mozzarella cheese

In an 8½-inch (22-cm) oven-safe skillet, heat 2 teaspoons (10 ml) of the olive oil over medium heat. Place the zucchini wedges in an even layer in the pan and cook them on all sides until they're lightly golden, 2 to 3 minutes per side. Transfer the zucchini to a plate lined with a paper towel.

In the same pan, combine the garlic, Italian seasoning, salt, crushed tomatoes and water. Bring it to a simmer, add the penne and stir. Cook the penne in the sauce for 15 to 20 minutes, stirring frequently, until it's tender. Place the zucchini in the pan with the pasta and stir to coat it in the sauce.

Preheat the broiler with the oven rack about 6 inches (15 cm) below the heating element.

In a small bowl, combine the bread crumbs, salt, the remaining 1 teaspoon olive oil and the Parmesan cheese. Top the zucchini and pasta with the mozzarella cheese and sprinkle the bread crumbs over the top. Place the skillet under the broiler in the oven for 5 minutes, or until the bread crumbs are crispy and the cheese has melted.

Pork Chops *with* Savory Apple Bacon Hash

A hash, which is a combination of meat, potatoes and vegetables, is a great way to use up leftovers in the refrigerator. In this case, russet potatoes, apple and fresh chives cook together in a skillet along with some bacon and a thin-sliced pork chop.

Serves 1

1 slice thick-cut bacon, sliced into ½" (1.3-cm) pieces

1 (4-oz [115-g]) boneless pork chop, sliced in half horizontally

1 tbsp (14 g) unsalted butter

¼ cup (38 g) chopped red onion

1 tsp chopped garlic

1 cup (200 g) finely diced russet potato

1 cup (151 g) finely diced Granny Smith apple

½ tsp kosher salt

1 tbsp (15 ml) apple cider vinegar

1 tsp chopped fresh chives, for garnish

In an 8½-inch (22-cm) skillet, cook the bacon over medium-low heat until it's rendered its fat. Move the bacon to the edge of the pan and brown the pork chops in the bacon fat for 2 to 3 minutes on each side. Remove the pork chops from the pan.

Add the butter to the pan with the bacon and, once it's melted, turn the heat to medium and add the onion, garlic and potatoes. Stir the vegetables to coat them in the butter and cook them for 5 minutes, stirring occasionally. Add the diced apple and salt and stir, and cook it all for another 5 minutes.

Pour the vinegar into the pan and stir, scraping up any browned bits off the bottom of the pan. Spread the vegetables into an even layer and place the pork chops on top. Cover the pan with a lid and adjust the heat to medium-low. Cook the pork chops for 10 minutes, or until the internal temperature is 145°F (63°C). Garnish the pork chops with the chopped chives and serve.

Pan-Seared Sausage *with* White Beans *and* Broccolini

Broccolini is sold in small bunches and has a milder, sweeter taste than its cousin broccoli. While the broccolini cooks in the pan, it caramelizes in spots, which brings out its natural sweetness. For this recipe, trim the stems so they are of equal thickness to ensure they cook through quickly; combined with the sausage and white beans you'll have a quick and easy one-skillet dinner.

Serves 1

1 tbsp (15 ml) olive oil

1 (3-oz [85-g]) mild Italian sausage link, sliced into 1" (2.5-cm) pieces

4 oz (115 g) broccolini, stems trimmed

Juice of 1 lemon, divided

½ tsp kosher salt

½ cup (120 g) cannellini beans

In an 8½-inch (22-cm) skillet, heat the olive oil over medium heat. Add the sausage slices and brown them for 3 to 4 minutes per side. Transfer the sausage to a clean plate, leaving the fat in the pan.

Place the broccolini in the skillet and add the juice from ½ of the lemon. Cover the pan and cook the broccolini for 5 minutes, then flip it over and cook for another 5 minutes with the lid on. Uncover and add the juice from the other half of the lemon. Add the salt, beans and sausage and cook them for 2 to 3 minutes, or until the beans are warmed through.

Eggs *in* Spicy Tomatillo Sauce

Inspired by the many plates of huevos rancheros I enjoyed while living in New Mexico, these eggs in tomatillo sauce are a favorite easy dinner on nights when I want something quick. The eggs cook in the sauce just until the whites are set, so when you break the yolks they add richness to the bright and acidic sauce.

Serves 1

1 tsp olive oil

¼ cup (38 g) finely diced red onion

4 oz (115 g) tomatillos, paper husks removed, rinsed and chopped

1 tbsp (9 g) canned diced green chile

2 tsp (6 g) minced garlic

Juice from ½ lime

½ tsp kosher salt

2 tsp (2 g) chopped fresh cilantro

2 large eggs

2 (8" [20-cm]) flour tortillas, warmed

1 tbsp (8 g) crumbled queso fresco cheese (see note)

Heat the olive oil in an 8½-inch (22-cm) skillet over medium heat. Add the onion, tomatillos, green chile and garlic. Cook for 10 minutes, or until the tomatillos break down and release their moisture. Mash the tomatillos with a potato masher and add the lime juice, salt and cilantro and stir. Simmer for 5 minutes.

Crack the eggs into the sauce. Cover the skillet with a lid and cook the eggs for 5 minutes, or until the whites are set but the yolks are runny. Serve the sauce and eggs on the tortillas and top with the cheese.

NOTE: Queso fresco is a Mexican crumbling cheese that is available in most grocery stores, but feta cheese is a good substitute if you can't find queso fresco.

Spinach Pork Roulade *with* Prosciutto Arugula Salad

This spinach pork roulade is best described as faux-fancy, because it's easy to make and calls for simple ingredients, but the end result looks like something you might order in a restaurant. The pork is pounded thin, rolled up with some spinach and garlic, breaded and baked, and comes out of the oven juicy and full of flavor. Slice and serve it with a lightly dressed arugula salad and dinner is ready in less than an hour.

Serves 1

Pork

1 (5-oz [142-g]) boneless pork loin chop

2 pinches of kosher salt

2 tsp (10 ml) olive oil

2 tbsp (14 g) frozen chopped spinach (see note)

1 tsp minced garlic

1 tsp Dijon mustard

1 tbsp (14 g) mayonnaise, divided

2 tsp (5 g) grated Parmesan cheese

1 tbsp (8 g) fine bread crumbs, seasoned with 1 pinch of salt

Salad

¼ tsp Dijon mustard

1 pinch of kosher salt

1 tsp lemon juice

1 tsp olive oil

2 cups (40 g) fresh baby arugula

1 oz (28 g) thin-sliced prosciutto, cut into long strips

1 tbsp (11 g) grated Parmesan

Preheat the oven to 375°F (190°C).

To make the pork, place the pork on a cutting board and cover it with plastic wrap. Using a meat mallet, pound the pork until it's ⅛ inch (3 mm) thick. Season both sides of the pork with the salt.

In an 8½-inch (22-cm) ovenproof skillet, heat the olive oil over medium-low heat. Add the chopped spinach and coat it in the oil. Add the garlic and cover the pan. Cook the spinach for 3 minutes, or until it's thawed. Turn the heat off and keep the skillet covered while you prepare the pork.

Spread the mustard and half of the mayonnaise on one side of the pork. Spoon the spinach and garlic on top, scraping all of it out of the pan, and spread it into an even layer. Sprinkle the Parmesan cheese over the top.

Starting at one end, roll the pork into a log. Coat the outside of the pork with the rest of the mayonnaise. Roll the pork in the bread crumbs until it's evenly coated. Place the pork in the pan and transfer the pan to the oven. Bake it for 25 to 30 minutes, or until the internal temperature is 160°F (71°C). Remove from the oven, let rest, then slice crosswise into 1-inch (2.5-cm)-thick pinwheels.

While the pork is cooking, make the salad. Combine the mustard, salt, lemon juice and olive oil in a medium-size bowl. Place the arugula and prosciutto in the bowl and toss it with the dressing. Top with the grated Parmesan cheese. Serve alongside the pork.

NOTE: Using frozen chopped spinach in a bag makes it easy to portion out a small amount for recipes as opposed to spinach sold in 10-ounce (284-g) frozen blocks.

Potato, Bacon *and* Brie Frittata

This frittata borrows ingredients from a French dish called *tartiflette*, which is a hearty dish of potatoes, bacon and cheese with white wine. Here those ingredients are combined with eggs for a simple frittata.

Serves 1

1 slice thick-cut bacon, cut into 1" (2.5-cm) pieces

1 tbsp (14 g) unsalted butter

¼ cup (38 g) finely diced red onion

1 tsp minced garlic

1 cup (200 g) diced russet potatoes, cut into ¼" (6-mm) pieces

¼ tsp kosher salt

1 tbsp (15 ml) dry white wine

1 tsp chopped fresh chives

2 large eggs, beaten and seasoned with 1 pinch each of kosher salt and black pepper

1 (1-oz [28-g]) slice Brie, cut into 3 pieces

Preheat the oven to 350°F (175°C).

In an ovenproof 8½-inch (22-cm) nonstick skillet, cook the bacon over medium heat until it's rendered its fat. Add the butter, onion, garlic, potatoes and salt. Cook the vegetables, stirring occasionally, until the potatoes are fork tender. Pour the wine into the pan along with the chives. Stir and simmer until the wine is mostly evaporated from the pan.

Adjust the heat to medium-low and pour the eggs into the pan. Cook just until the eggs start to pull away from the edges of the pan. Top with the Brie and transfer the skillet to the oven. Bake the frittata for 10 to 15 minutes, or until the eggs are set in the center.

Beef Stroganoff *with* Toast

One of the first real dishes I learned to make, as a tenderhearted thirteen-year-old in home economics class, was beef stroganoff. It's a hearty beef and mushroom combo in a rich and savory sauce. Here I've scaled it down to serve one, with some toasted bread on the side to soak up all the sauce. It's a comforting one-skillet dinner.

Serves 1

1 tsp olive oil

4 oz (115 g) sirloin steak, seasoned on both sides with kosher salt

1 tbsp (14 g) unsalted butter

4 oz (115 g) whole button mushrooms

¼ cup (38 g) finely diced yellow onion

1 tsp minced garlic

1 tbsp (15 ml) dry white wine

2 tsp (5 g) all-purpose flour

¼ cup (60 ml) beef stock

1 tsp Dijon mustard

1 tbsp (8 g) sour cream

1 tsp chopped fresh parsley, for garnish

2 slices French bread, toasted

In an 8½-inch (22-cm) skillet, heat the olive oil over medium heat. Place the steak in the pan and cook it on one side until it's browned, about 5 minutes. Flip it over and brown it on the other side for another 3 to 4 minutes. Transfer the steak to a cutting board to rest for 1 to 2 minutes. Slice into ⅛-inch (3-mm)-thick slices.

In the same pan, melt the butter. Add the mushrooms and stir to coat them in the butter. Cook the mushrooms until they turn golden brown, about 5 minutes. Add the onion and garlic and cook them with the mushrooms for about 3 minutes, stirring frequently, until the onions soften. Add the wine and use your spatula or spoon to scrape up the browned bits off the bottom of the pan. Add the flour and stir until the vegetables are coated. Add the beef stock and mustard, stirring to combine, and bring the pan to a strong simmer. Cook until the sauce has thickened enough to coat the back of a spoon, about 5 minutes. Return the beef to the pan and cook for 1 minute.

Remove the pan from the heat and stir in the sour cream. Garnish with the chopped parsley and serve with the toasted bread.

Saucy Baked Ravioli

Store-bought fresh ravioli is one of my go-to easy dinner ingredients, and my favorite way to use it is in a saucy baked pasta dish that starts on the stovetop and goes straight into the oven in the same skillet. This ravioli is cooked in a simple tomato sauce with fresh rosemary and balsamic vinegar—no need to boil the pasta separately.

Serves 2

2 tsp (10 ml) olive oil

¼ cup (38 g) chopped yellow onion

1 tbsp (10 g) minced garlic

1 tsp finely chopped fresh rosemary

½ tsp kosher salt

1 pinch of black pepper

1 tbsp (15 ml) balsamic vinegar

1 cup (242 g) crushed tomatoes

¼ cup (60 ml) water

2 cups (115 g) store-bought fresh cheese ravioli

⅓ cup (40 g) shredded mozzarella cheese

¼ cup (33 g) shredded Asiago cheese

1 tsp chopped fresh parsley, for garnish

Preheat the oven to 350°F (175°C).

In an 8½-inch (22-cm) ovenproof skillet, heat the olive oil over medium heat. Add the onions, garlic and rosemary and stir and cook them for 1 minute, or until the herbs and garlic are fragrant. Add the salt, pepper, vinegar, tomatoes and water. Stir and adjust the heat to bring the sauce to a simmer. Add the ravioli and stir it into the sauce.

Top the pasta and sauce with the mozzarella and Asiago cheese. Cover the skillet loosely with foil and transfer it to the oven. Bake the ravioli for 15 minutes. Remove the foil and bake the ravioli for 10 minutes uncovered, or until the sauce is bubbling and the ravioli is cooked through. Let the ravioli stand for a few minutes. Garnish with the parsley and serve.

Shrimp Puttanesca *with* Lima Beans

Puttanesca is a classic Italian dish that is full of fresh flavor with a briny bite from olives and capers. This version includes some lima beans, but you can also use cannellini beans. As the tomatoes cook, their juices create a light sauce flavored with the olives, capers and garlic. Although it's traditionally served with pasta, I like to serve it straight from the skillet with just some toast.

Serves 1

2 tsp (10 ml) olive oil

1 cup (150 g) cherry tomatoes, halved

2 tsp (6 g) minced garlic

¼ cup (30 g) chopped pitted Kalamata olives

1 tsp roughly chopped capers

½ cup (120 g) canned lima beans, drained and rinsed

½ tsp kosher salt

4 oz (115 g) shrimp, 51/60 count size, peeled, deveined and tails removed

1 tbsp (3 g) sliced fresh basil

1 tbsp (3 g) chopped fresh parsley

1 slice country bread, toasted and cut in half, for serving (optional)

In an 8½-inch (22-cm) skillet, heat the olive oil over medium heat. Add the tomatoes and cook them for 1 minute, or until they start to break down and release their juices. Add the garlic, olives, capers, beans and salt. Stir and cook for 1 minute.

Add the shrimp and stir to combine. Cover the pan with a lid and cook the shrimp for 2 minutes. Uncover and add the basil and parsley. Stir to combine and cook for another 3 to 4 minutes, or until the shrimp are opaque and cooked through. Serve with toast, if desired.

Skillet Eggplant *with* Sausage, Kale *and* Orzo

Look for a small eggplant (often called Italian or baby eggplant) to make this recipe. The skin is thinner, which means you don't need to peel it, and the flavor is less bitter, which means you don't need to salt and drain the slices before cooking. Since orzo is a very small pasta that looks like rice, it gives this dish some texture without making it a full-on "pasta" recipe.

Serves 2

1 tbsp (15 ml) olive oil

1 (8-oz [227-g]) baby eggplant, halved lengthwise and sliced into 1" (2.5-cm) half-moons

1 (3-oz [85-g]) Italian sausage link, casing removed

Juice of 1 lemon, divided

4 oz (115 g) fresh kale, stems and ribs removed and roughly chopped

½ tsp kosher salt

1½ cups (355 ml) water

¼ cup (40 g) orzo

1 tbsp (3 g) chopped fresh parsley

¼ cup (38 g) crumbled feta cheese

In a 10-inch (25-cm) skillet, heat the olive oil over medium heat. Place the eggplant slices in a single layer in the pan and cook them until they're lightly golden, 1 to 2 minutes on each side. Transfer the eggplant to a plate. In the same pan, cook the sausage until it's browned, breaking it apart with a spatula as it cooks, 3 to 4 minutes. Add the juice from half of the lemon and, as it simmers, scrape up any browned bits off the bottom of the pan.

Add the kale to the pan and stir until it wilts, 2 to 3 minutes. Add the salt, water and remaining lemon juice. Bring the liquid to a simmer, add the orzo and parsley and stir to combine. Add the eggplant slices back to the skillet and lower the heat if needed to maintain a simmer while the orzo cooks. Stir frequently so the orzo does not stick to the pan and simmer until the liquid has reduced and the orzo is tender, 10 to 12 minutes. Top each serving with crumbled feta cheese.

"Milk Can Dinner"

Growing up in Wyoming I used to attend these mysterious events called "Milk Can Dinners," where myriad ingredients like chicken, corn, potatoes and beer would go into large milk cans that were placed over a flame. After all the ingredients simmered together, what emerged was a cornucopia of summertime deliciousness that fed a lot of people. For our purposes we're skipping the milk can part and cooking everything together in a foil packet. This is a low-fuss, easy-cleanup dinner.

Serves 1

¼ small red onion, sliced into wedges

½ tsp chili powder

½ tsp paprika

½ tsp garlic powder

½ tsp onion powder

½ tsp kosher salt

1 pinch of black pepper

5 oz (142 g) petite red potatoes, cut into 1" (2.5-cm) pieces

2 tsp (10 ml) olive oil, divided

1 (6-oz [170-g]) boneless, skinless chicken breast

1 small (6" [15-cm]) ear of corn, husk and silk removed and cut in half

1 tbsp (15 ml) Mexican-style beer

1 tbsp (14 g) unsalted butter, divided

1 tbsp (3 g) chopped fresh parsley

Preheat the oven to 400°F (200°C). Line a baking sheet with a large piece of foil.

Place the onion in the center of the foil. Combine the chili powder, paprika, garlic powder, onion powder, salt and pepper in a small bowl. Place the potatoes in a medium bowl. Toss them with 1 teaspoon of the olive oil and half of the spice mixture. Place the potatoes on top of the onions. Coat the chicken breast with the remaining 1 teaspoon olive oil and the rest of the spices. Place the chicken on top of the potatoes with both pieces of corn.

Pull the ends and sides of the foil up around the chicken and vegetables into a packet shape, leaving an opening to add the rest of the ingredients. Add the beer to the packet, top each piece of corn with the butter (½ tablespoon [7 g] each) and sprinkle the parsley over the top. Seal the packet by folding the ends and sides of the foil together, leaving some space for air to circulate. Transfer the baking sheet to the oven and bake it for 35 to 40 minutes, or until the internal temperature of the chicken is 165°F (74°C).

Sheet-Pan Cod *with* Roasted Red Potatoes

I was hesitant to share that the inspiration for this easy sheet-pan dinner was fish and chips because I removed many steps from the classic version, but that's where it began. Instead of deep-fried cod, this dish features a simple breaded fillet baked alongside red potatoes seasoned with pantry spices. It's less greasy and easier to make, but in the same spirit as traditional fish and chips.

Serves 1

5 oz (142 g) petite red potatoes, quartered

1 tsp olive oil

¼ tsp paprika

½ tsp garlic powder

½ tsp kosher salt

¼ tsp black pepper

1 (4-oz [115-g]) cod fillet, seasoned with salt and pepper

1 tsp mayonnaise

2 tsp (5 g) fine bread crumbs

1 tsp chopped fresh parsley, for garnish

2 lemon wedges, for serving

Preheat the oven to 400°F (200°C). Line a baking sheet with foil.

Place the potatoes on the sheet pan. Drizzle the olive oil over the top of the potatoes and sprinkle the paprika, garlic powder, salt and pepper over the top. Gently toss the potatoes to coat them evenly in the oil and spices. Transfer the potatoes to the oven and roast them for 10 minutes.

While the potatoes roast, prepare the fish. Coat one side of the fish with the mayonnaise, then sprinkle the bread crumbs over it and gently press them into the mayonnaise.

After the potatoes have roasted for 10 minutes, remove the baking sheet from the oven. Turn the potatoes with a spatula and move them to one side of the pan. Place the fish, bread-crumb-side up, on the baking sheet. Return the baking sheet to the oven and roast the potatoes and fish for 10 to 15 minutes, or until the fish easily flakes with a fork and the potatoes are fork tender. Sprinkle with the parsley and serve with the lemon wedges on the side.

One-Pan Chipotle Macaroni Beef

This simple skillet dinner is all about comfort. Inspired by the American-style goulash I ate growing up, this combination of ground beef, carrots and pasta cooked in a chipotle pepper sauce gives that childhood favorite a spicy upgrade. For an extra kick, double the amount of chipotle pepper.

Serves 1

1 tsp olive oil

4 oz (115 g) ground beef

¼ cup (38 g) finely chopped onion

¼ cup (32 g) finely diced carrot

½ tsp kosher salt

Pinch of black pepper

1 tsp finely chopped chipotle pepper

2 tbsp (30 ml) adobo sauce

1¼ cups (296 ml) beef broth

2 oz (60 g) macaroni

Juice of 1 lime

1 tsp chopped fresh cilantro

1 tbsp (8 g) sour cream

In an 8½-inch (22-cm) skillet, heat the olive oil over medium heat. Place the beef in the pan and cook it, breaking it apart with your spatula, until it's no longer pink, 3 to 4 minutes. Add the onion, carrot, salt, pepper, chipotle pepper and adobo sauce and stir to combine.

Add the beef broth and stir. Bring the pan to a boil and add the macaroni. Adjust the heat to maintain a simmer and cook the pasta for 10 minutes, stirring frequently. Add the lime juice and cilantro and cook for 5 minutes, or until the pasta is tender and most of the liquid has been absorbed. Turn off the heat, add the sour cream and serve.

Skillet Chorizo Rice *with* Sweet Potatoes

Spanish chorizo is a cured pork sausage that comes in both spicy and mild varieties. Because it's already cooked it only needs a few minutes in a hot pan to extract some of its fat. For this recipe, sweet potatoes and rice cook in the flavorful fat along with fresh lemon before you add the chorizo back in; because of the chorizo's strong flavor, you don't need a lot of extra ingredients, making this an easy skillet dinner.

Serves 1

2 tsp (10 ml) olive oil

2 oz (60 g) grated Spanish chorizo

1 cup (200 g) finely diced sweet potato

1 tsp minced garlic

Juice of 1 lemon

½ tsp kosher salt

¼ tsp ground black pepper

1¼ cups (296 ml) water

¼ cup (53 g) long-grain white rice

1 tbsp (3 g) chopped fresh parsley, divided

In a 10-inch (25-cm) skillet, heat the olive oil over medium heat. Add the chorizo and cook it in the oil for 2 to 3 minutes, or until it starts to release some fat. Remove to a clean plate. Add the potatoes and garlic to the pan and cook them in the fat until the potatoes start to brown, about 5 minutes. Add the lemon juice and scrape up the browned bits off the bottom of the pan. Add the salt and pepper and stir.

Pour the water into the pan and bring it to a boil. Add the rice, stir and cover the pan with a lid. Simmer the rice for 10 to 15 minutes, or until the liquid has reduced by half. Uncover the pan, add ½ tablespoon (1.5 g) of the chopped parsley and continue to simmer, stirring frequently, until the rice has absorbed all of the liquid and is tender, 5 to 10 minutes. Add the chorizo back to the pan and stir. Garnish with the remaining ½ tablespoon (1.5 g) parsley and serve.

Pecan-Encrusted Salmon
with Roasted Asparagus

Sheet pans make for easy dinners that don't leave you with a pile of dishes in the sink. Load that sheet pan up with fresh asparagus and salmon topped with a pecan–bread crumb crust and you have the makings for a fast and light dinner.

Serves 1

6 oz (170 g) asparagus, ends trimmed

2 tsp (10 ml) olive oil, divided

¼ tsp ground black pepper

¾ tsp kosher salt, divided

¼ cup (30 g) finely chopped pecans

1 tbsp (8 g) bread crumbs

1 tsp lemon zest

½ tsp dried oregano

4 oz (115 g) salmon fillet, lightly coated with olive oil

1 lemon wedge, for serving

Preheat the oven to 400°F (200°C).

Spread the asparagus in an even layer on one half of a baking sheet. Drizzle 1 teaspoon of the olive oil over the top and gently toss the asparagus to coat it evenly in the oil. Season the asparagus with the black pepper and ¼ teaspoon of the salt.

In a small bowl, combine the pecans, bread crumbs, zest, oregano, remaining ½ teaspoon salt and remaining 1 teaspoon olive oil. Place the salmon skin-side down on the baking sheet and top it with the pecan mixture, gently pressing on the salmon to form a crust. Transfer the baking sheet to the oven and roast the salmon and asparagus for 15 minutes, or until the salmon easily flakes with a fork and the asparagus is tender. Squeeze the lemon wedge over the top of the salmon and asparagus and serve.

Two-Serving Soups, Stews and Chilis

Some people are good at making a big batch of soup and freezing it in perfectly portioned containers, each properly labeled with the contents and date they were made. From there those people admirably thaw and reheat the leftover soup and are happy to eat the same thing over and over again.

I am not one of those people. But I am a person who loves the process of soup-making, so I needed to find a way to enjoy the therapeutic act of simmering and stirring a pot of comforting goodness without the nagging guilt of leftovers languishing in the dark recesses of the freezer only to be tossed out months later. So it was my acceptance of my inept freezer organization skills and my aversion to eating the same thing over and over again that led to a love of making small-batch soups.

Each of the recipes that follow stands on its own as dinner, whether it's the hearty Red Wine Beef Stew (page 168), the simple Pinto Bean Chili with Avocado Quesadillas on the side (page 167) or the elegant, cheese plate–inspired White Cheddar Soup with Pear and Almond Salad combination (page 155). These two-serving soups, stews and chilis are not only easier to make than their big-batch inspirations (less chopping and dicing!), but they're also enjoyable hot from the stove without the worry of how you might store a vast quantity of leftovers. In other words, all of the soup-making fun without the guilt.

Tuscan-Style White Bean Soup

Sometimes less is more, and as with this weeknight-friendly soup, you don't always need a bunch of ingredients to create a satisfying dinner. This is a lesson I learned while eating my way through Italy, and this Tuscan-inspired soup with creamy white beans, fresh herbs and tomato-based broth spiked with a splash of tangy balsamic pays humble respect to that philosophy of cooking. Pair the soup with some crusty bread on the side to soak up every last drop.

Serves 2

1 tbsp (15 ml) olive oil

½ cup (76 g) finely chopped red onion

1 tbsp (10 g) minced garlic

1 tbsp (15 ml) balsamic vinegar

2 tbsp (33 g) tomato paste

1½ tsp (9 g) kosher salt

1 (15-oz [425-g]) can cannellini beans, drained and rinsed

2½ cups (592 ml) vegetable stock

2 large basil leaves, sliced into thin ribbons

1 tsp Parmesan cheese, for serving

In a 3½-quart (3-L) saucepan, heat the olive oil over medium heat. Add the onions and garlic and cook them in the oil, stirring frequently, for 2 to 3 minutes or until they start to soften. Add the vinegar and stir to coat the vegetables. Add the tomato paste and salt and stir again until the tomato paste evenly coats the vegetables.

Add the beans and vegetable stock. Bring the soup to a boil, then reduce the heat to maintain a gentle simmer. Simmer the soup for 15 minutes. Using a potato masher, mash some of the beans to thicken the soup, leaving some beans whole. Simmer the soup for 5 minutes. Sprinkle with the basil and Parmesan and serve.

White Cheddar Soup *with* Pear *and* Almond Salad

Inspired by my love of cheese plates, I took the main parts—in this case, aged white cheddar cheese, fresh fruit and nuts—and turned them into a soup and salad combo. The creamy, rich white cheddar soup is complemented by a cool arugula salad with fresh pear slices and crunchy almonds. Add your favorite crisp white wine to make this meal complete—just as you would with a cheese plate.

Serves 2

Soup

2 tbsp (28 g) butter

½ cup (76 g) finely chopped yellow onion

2 tsp (6 g) minced garlic

2 tbsp (16 g) all-purpose flour

1 cup (235 ml) vegetable stock

¾ cup (180 ml) 2% milk

½ tsp kosher salt

1 tbsp (3 g) chopped fresh parsley

1 cup (115 g) shredded aged white cheddar cheese

Salad

4 cups (80 g) baby arugula

Juice from ½ lemon

2 tsp (10 ml) olive oil

1 (9-oz [255-g]) Bartlett pear, cored and sliced into ¼" (6-mm) slices

¼ cup (30 g) slivered almonds

1 tbsp (3 g) chopped fresh parsley

To make the soup, melt the butter in a 3½-quart (3-L) saucepan over medium heat. Add the onion and cook it in the butter for 5 minutes, or until it's softened. Add the garlic and cook it for 1 minute or just until it's fragrant. Add the flour and stir until it is combined with the butter and onions. Slowly add the vegetable stock, stirring continuously, until it starts to thicken. Reduce the heat to medium-low and slowly add the milk, stirring until the soup is smooth. Cook the soup for 5 minutes over medium-low heat.

Add the salt and parsley to the soup and stir. Add half of the cheese and stir until it's melted. Add the rest of the cheese and stir until it's melted and the soup is smooth. Turn the heat to low to keep the soup warm while you make the salad.

To make the salad, place the arugula in a medium-size bowl. Drizzle the lemon juice and olive oil over the top and gently toss the arugula to coat it evenly in the dressing. Pile the arugula on a plate and tuck the slices of pear into it. Sprinkle the almonds and parsley over the top. Serve the salad with bowls of soup on the side.

NOTE: Look for slivered almonds in the baking aisle, where you can buy them already slivered and packaged in small amounts.

Cilantro–Lime Chicken Rice Soup

This cilantro–lime chicken rice soup is a seasonal gateway soup that combines summer flavors like sweet corn, earthy poblano pepper and fresh cilantro with a warmth and heartiness that will warm you up on a crisp fall day.

Serves 2

2 tsp (10 ml) olive oil

1 (1-lb [454-g]) skin-on, bone-in chicken breast, seasoned with salt

¾ cup (114 g) chopped yellow onion

½ cup (90 g) finely diced poblano pepper

2 tsp (7 g) finely chopped garlic

1 cup (165 g) frozen corn kernels

4 cups (945 ml) chicken stock, divided

½ cup (105 g) long-grain white rice

Juice from 1 lime

1 tbsp (3 g) chopped fresh cilantro

Salt, to taste

In a 3½-quart (3-L) saucepan, heat the olive oil over medium heat. Place the chicken skin-side down in the pan to brown the skin, 5 to 10 minutes. Once browned, remove the chicken from the pan to a cutting board.

In the same pan, add the onion and pepper and cook them over medium heat. As they release their moisture, scrape up any browned bits off the bottom of the pan. Add the garlic and corn. Cook them for 1 to 2 minutes before adding 3 cups (710 ml) of the chicken stock. Bring the soup to a boil, then reduce the heat to medium-low to maintain a simmer. Place the chicken in the soup, skin-side down. Simmer the chicken for 15 minutes. Turn the chicken over in the soup and simmer it for 15 minutes.

Transfer the chicken to a cutting board. Add the rice to the soup and adjust the heat so the soup is lightly simmering. While the rice and soup simmer, shred the chicken with two forks and discard the skin and bones. Roughly chop the meat into bite-size pieces. Add the shredded chicken back to the soup and stir. As the rice absorbs the liquid, add as much of the remaining 1 cup (235 ml) chicken stock as needed to thin the soup. Add the lime juice and cilantro. Add salt to taste. Simmer for 1 minute and serve.

French Onion Chicken Soup

If you're going to spend the time to make French onion soup—an endeavor that pays dividends in its rewards—it's good form to add some roast chicken to take it from a light supper to a filling dinner. In the time it takes to caramelize the onions, you can roast the chicken, and from there it's as simple as simmering the soup to marry all of the flavors. Use oven-safe bowls for the grand finale—soup topped with toasted bread and melted Gruyère cheese—and you might think your kitchen has transformed into a quaint French bistro.

Serves 2

2 tbsp (28 g) unsalted butter

1 (1-lb [454-g]) white onion, peeled and sliced into ⅛" (3-mm) slices

½ tsp kosher salt

1 (8-oz [225-g]) skin-on, bone-in chicken thigh, seasoned with kosher salt

1 tsp olive oil

1 tbsp (15 ml) dry white wine

2 cups (470 ml) chicken stock

1 bay leaf

1 tsp Herbes de Provence

¼ tsp black pepper

1 tbsp (16 g) Dijon mustard

2 slices French bread (cut to fit the top of the serving bowl), toasted

½ cup (56 g) shredded Gruyère cheese

Preheat the oven to 400°F (200°C).

In a 3½-quart (3-L) saucepan, melt the butter over medium heat. Add the onions and stir to coat them in the butter, add the salt, adjust the heat to low and cook the onions, stirring occasionally, for 45 to 60 minutes, or until they are softened and caramelized.

While the onions cook, place the chicken on a baking sheet and coat it in the olive oil. Roast the chicken for 30 minutes, or until the internal temperature is 165°F (74°C). Remove the chicken from the oven and let it rest for 5 minutes. Remove the meat from the bone and shred it. Discard the skin and bones.

When the onions are caramelized, turn the heat to medium and add the wine to the pan. As it simmers, stir the onions until the wine has mostly evaporated, about 1 minute. Add the shredded chicken to the pan and stir. Add the chicken stock, bay leaf, Herbes de Provence and black pepper. Stir and bring the soup to a boil and then reduce the heat to medium-low. Simmer the soup for 15 minutes.

Turn the broiler on and place two oven-safe soup bowls on a sheet pan. Divide the mustard between the toasted bread slices and spread it in an even layer on each.

Remove the bay leaf from the soup and discard it. Ladle the soup into the bowls and top each bowl with a piece of toasted bread with the mustard side up. Top each piece of bread with the cheese. Transfer the soup to the oven and broil until the cheese is melted, 3 to 5 minutes.

Smoky Bacon Mushroom Soup

These days you can find a variety of mushrooms at the grocery store, which is good news for mushroom soup. Shiitake mushrooms, with their robust flavor, serve as both the base and the garnish for this creamy soup made with bacon and white wine.

Serves 2

4 oz (115 g) shiitake mushrooms, stemmed and sliced

1 slice thick-cut bacon, cut into 1" (2.5-cm) pieces

¼ cup (38 g) chopped red onion

2 tsp (6 g) chopped garlic

1 tsp kosher salt

1 tbsp (15 ml) dry white wine

2¼ cups (532 ml) vegetable stock

1 tbsp (3 g) chopped fresh parsley, divided

¼ cup (60 ml) heavy cream

First, pick out 8 mushroom slices and set them aside for the garnish. Roughly chop the rest of the mushrooms and set aside.

In a 3½-quart (3-L) saucepan, cook the bacon over medium heat until it's crispy, 2 to 3 minutes per side. Remove half of the bacon to a plate lined with a paper towel. Transfer half the bacon fat to an 8½-inch (22-cm) nonstick skillet that you will use to prepare the garnish after you've made the soup.

Add the onions to the saucepan with the reserved bacon and bacon fat. Cook the onions over medium heat until they start to soften, 2 to 3 minutes. Add the garlic, chopped mushrooms and salt and cook them for 10 minutes, or until the mushrooms release their moisture. Add the wine and simmer for 1 minute. Add the vegetable stock, bring the soup to a boil and reduce the heat to medium-low to maintain a simmer. Simmer the soup while you make the garnish.

To make the garnish, heat the reserved bacon fat in the nonstick skillet over medium heat. Fry the sliced mushrooms until they are golden and crispy on both sides, 1 to 2 minutes per side. Transfer the mushrooms to a plate lined with a paper towel. Finely chop the cooked bacon that you set aside earlier to use for garnish.

Puree the soup using an immersion blender until it is smooth. Add half of the chopped parsley and all of the cream to the soup. To serve, ladle the soup into bowls and top with the crispy mushrooms, chopped bacon and the remaining parsley.

Roasted Cauliflower Soup *and* Cranberry Turkey Grilled Cheese

This recipe is like Thanksgiving dinner in soup and sandwich form, complete with homemade cranberry sauce, turkey and a mashed potato–inspired creamy cauliflower soup. And as with any great soup and grilled cheese combo, don't be afraid to do a little sandwich dunking for the best experience.

Serves 2

Soup
1 (10-oz [284-g]) head cauliflower, broken into 1" (2.5-cm) florets

1½ tbsp (22 ml) olive oil, divided

2 tsp (10 g) kosher salt, divided

½ cup (76 g) chopped onion

2 tsp (6 g) chopped garlic

½ tsp dried oregano

2½ cups (592 ml) vegetable stock

Juice from ½ lemon

⅓ cup (80 ml) heavy cream

1 tsp chopped fresh parsley, for garnish

Grilled Cheese
½ cup (50 g) frozen cranberries

Juice from ½ lemon

1 tbsp (15 ml) honey

2 tbsp (28 g) mayonnaise

2 tsp (10 g) Dijon mustard

4 slices country white bread

4 oz (115 g) thin-sliced deli turkey

4 slices Swiss cheese

2 tbsp (28 g) butter

Preheat the oven to 400°F (200°C).

To make the soup, spread the cauliflower florets in an even layer on a baking sheet. Coat the cauliflower evenly with 1 tablespoon (15 ml) of the olive oil and season it with 1 teaspoon of the salt. Roast the cauliflower for 15 minutes. Use a spatula to flip the cauliflower over on the sheet pan and continue to roast it for another 15 minutes, or until it's fork tender.

In a 3½-quart (3-L) saucepan, heat the remaining ½ tablespoon (7 ml) olive oil over medium heat. Add the onions and cook them for 5 minutes, stirring occasionally. Add the garlic, the remaining 1 teaspoon salt and the oregano and stir. Add the roasted cauliflower and vegetable stock and bring the soup to a boil. Reduce the heat to medium-low and simmer the soup for 10 minutes. Puree the soup using an immersion blender, add the lemon juice and simmer it over medium-low heat while you make the grilled cheese sandwiches.

To make the sandwiches, first cook the frozen cranberries and lemon juice in a small saucepan over medium heat. Once the cranberries have warmed through, add the honey. Stir to combine and use a potato masher to mash the cranberries. Cook the sauce for 1 minute, or until it has thickened. Remove the saucepan from the heat and set aside.

Divide the mayonnaise and mustard between 2 bread slices and spread them into an even layer on each. Top the bread with the turkey and 2 slices of cheese for each sandwich. Spread the cranberry sauce on the other 2 slices of bread.

Melt the butter in a medium-size nonstick skillet over medium heat. Place the sandwiches in the pan. Cook on each side for 3 to 4 minutes, or until the cheese has melted and the bread is golden and crispy.

Add the cream to the soup and stir to combine. Serve the soup, sprinkled with the parsley, with the sandwiches on the side.

Sweet Potato Soup *with* Shrimp *and* Corn Garnish

I love a great soup garnish. It's often what takes a simple bowl of soup that you might consider an appetizer or light lunch and transforms it into something not just more satisfying but more beautiful as well. In this case, the light and fresh flavor of the shrimp and corn is a lovely complement to the rich and creamy potato soup flavored with a touch of smoky bacon and fresh herbs.

Serves 2

Soup

1 slice thick-cut bacon

½ cup (76 g) finely chopped onion, cut into ¼" (6-mm) pieces

2 tsp (6 g) minced garlic

12 oz (340 g) sweet potatoes, peeled and cut into ½" (1.3-cm) pieces

Leaves from 3 sprigs fresh thyme

½ tsp kosher salt

¼ tsp black pepper

2½ cups (592 ml) vegetable stock

1 tsp apple cider vinegar

¼ cup (60 ml) heavy cream

Garnish

6 oz (170 g) shrimp, 31/40 count size, peeled and deveined

½ tsp chili powder

1 pinch of kosher salt

1 tsp olive oil

1 cup (165 g) frozen corn kernels, thawed

1 tsp chopped fresh parsley

To make the soup, cook the bacon in a 3-quart (3-L) saucepan over medium heat until it's crispy, 2 to 3 minutes per side. Transfer the bacon, leaving the fat in the pan, to a plate lined with a paper towel.

In the same pan, cook the onion and garlic in the bacon fat for 2 to 3 minutes, or until they soften. Add the potatoes, thyme, salt and pepper. Stir and cook the potatoes for 5 minutes. Add the vegetable stock and bring the soup to a boil. Adjust the heat to maintain a simmer and cook for 10 to 15 minutes, or until the potatoes are fork tender. While the soup simmers, finely chop the cooked bacon and set it aside. Puree the soup with an immersion blender until it's smooth and simmer it over medium-low heat while you make the garnish.

To make the garnish, season the shrimp with the chili powder and salt. Heat the olive oil in an 8½-inch (22-cm) skillet over medium heat. Add the corn and spread it into an even layer in the pan. Cook it without stirring for 2 to 3 minutes, then stir the kernels and cook them for another 3 minutes, or until they've taken on a light golden color. Push the kernels to the edge of the pan. Place the shrimp in the pan and cook them for 3 minutes. Flip them over and cook them for another 2 to 3 minutes, or until they are pink and opaque.

Add the vinegar and cream to the soup and stir to combine. Ladle the soup into bowls and garnish with the shrimp, corn, chopped parsley and chopped bacon.

Pinto Bean Chili *with* Avocado Quesadillas

This pinto bean chili puts your pantry to good use, and tastes like it cooked all day—but instead comes together in less than an hour. While the chili simmers, make the avocado quesadillas, also known as the best chili-dunking companion.

Serves 2

Chili

1 tbsp (15 ml) olive oil

½ cup (76 g) chopped red onion

2 tsp (6 g) minced garlic

½ cup (90 g) diced red bell pepper

1 jalapeño, diced

1 tbsp (8 g) chili powder

1 tsp ground cumin

1 tsp kosher salt

½ tsp paprika

¼ tsp black pepper

½ tbsp (9 g) tomato paste

1 (15-oz [425-g]) can diced tomatoes with juices

1 (15-oz [425-g]) can pinto beans, drained and rinsed

2 cups (470 ml) vegetable stock

2 tsp (2 g) chopped fresh cilantro

Juice from ½ lime

Quesadillas

1 small avocado, pitted and peeled

Juice from ½ lime

1 pinch of kosher salt

2 tsp (2 g) chopped fresh cilantro

2 (8" [20-cm]) flour tortillas

½ cup (65 g) shredded pepper Jack cheese

½ tsp olive oil

To make the chili, heat the olive oil in a 3½-quart (3-L) saucepan over medium heat. Add the onion, garlic, bell pepper and jalapeño. Cook the vegetables for 10 minutes, or until they release their moisture. Add the chili powder, cumin, salt, paprika, pepper and tomato paste. Stir to coat the vegetables in the spices. Add the tomatoes, beans and vegetable stock and turn the heat to high to bring it to a boil. Lower the heat to medium to maintain a strong simmer. Simmer the chili for 30 minutes.

To make the quesadillas, mash the avocado with the lime juice, salt and cilantro in a small bowl. Spread half of the avocado on a tortilla, leaving space around the edge. Top the avocado with half of the cheese and fold the tortilla in half. Repeat the same process with the second tortilla.

In a 10-inch (25-cm) nonstick skillet, heat the olive oil over medium heat. Cook the quesadillas until golden on both sides, 3 to 4 minutes total. Remove the quesadillas from the pan and slice each in half.

Add the cilantro and lime juice to the chili and serve it with the quesadillas on the side.

Red Wine Beef Stew

As much as I love eating a big hearty bowl of stew, I find the process of making stew equally as enjoyable. Chopping vegetables and simmering a pot of comforting goodness does wonders for the mind and spirit. The process can't be rushed, so it's a great excuse to slow down for a bit, and the reward is a bowl of tender beef and vegetables slow simmered in red wine, fresh herbs and mushrooms.

Serves 2

1 slice thick-cut bacon, cut into 1" (2.5-cm) pieces

8 oz (225 g) cubed stew meat

1 tsp kosher salt, divided

1 tbsp (8 g) flour

½ cup (76 g) finely chopped red onion

2 tsp (6 g) chopped garlic

1¼ cups (115 g) finely chopped white mushrooms

1 tbsp (16 g) tomato paste

1 cup (235 ml) cabernet sauvignon wine

3 cups (710 ml) beef stock

1 bay leaf

1 tsp fresh thyme leaves

8 oz (225 g) carrots, sliced into ½" (1.3-cm) coins

8 oz (225 g) Yukon gold potatoes, sliced into 1" (2.5-cm) pieces

1 tbsp (3 g) chopped fresh parsley

In a 3½-quart (3-L) saucepan over medium heat, cook the bacon until it releases its fat, 2 to 3 minutes per side. While the bacon cooks, place the beef cubes in a medium-size bowl. Season them with ½ teaspoon of the salt and toss them with the flour until they're evenly coated. Once the bacon has released its fat and starts to turn crispy, move it away from the center of the pan. Place the beef cubes in the pan and brown them on both sides, 3 to 4 minutes per side. Transfer the beef and bacon to a plate.

In the same pan, cook the onions until they start to release their moisture, about 5 minutes. Stir them around, scraping up the browned bits on the bottom of the pan. Add the garlic, mushrooms and remaining ½ teaspoon salt and stir to combine. Cook the mushrooms with the onion and garlic for 10 minutes, or until they've released most of their moisture. Add the tomato paste and stir to coat the vegetables. Add the wine, beef stock, bay leaf, thyme, bacon and beef. Cover and bring the stew to a boil and then reduce the heat to low and simmer for 1 hour uncovered, stirring occasionally.

Add the carrots and potatoes to the pan and simmer the stew for 1 hour, or until the potatoes and carrots are fork tender and the stew has thickened. Remove the bay leaf, add the chopped parsley and serve.

Spicy Sausage Pepper Soup

This spicy sausage pepper soup is a tip-of-the-hat to traditional oven-baked stuffed peppers. With Italian sausage, fresh bell pepper and tender rice that cooks right in the soup, it's as hearty as the dish that inspired it.

Serves 2

2 tsp (10 ml) olive oil

2 (3-oz [85-g]) hot Italian sausage links, casings removed

½ cup (76 g) finely chopped yellow onion

¾ cup (85 g) finely diced green bell pepper

1 tsp minced garlic

1 tsp dried oregano

1 tsp kosher salt

¼ tsp black pepper

1 tbsp (15 ml) balsamic vinegar

1 cup (240 ml) tomato sauce

4 cups (946 ml) water

½ cup (105 g) long-grain white rice

2 tbsp (22 g) grated Parmesan or Asiago cheese, for garnish

In a 3-quart (3-L) saucepan, heat the olive oil over medium heat. Brown the sausage for 4 to 5 minutes and break it apart as it cooks. Add the onion, bell pepper, garlic, oregano, salt and pepper. Stir to combine.

Add the balsamic and stir, scraping up any browned bits off the bottom of the pan. Add the tomato sauce and water to the pan. Adjust the heat to high and bring the soup to a boil. Add the rice and stir. Adjust the heat to medium and simmer the rice in the soup for 20 minutes, or until the rice is tender. Garnish each serving with cheese.

NOTES: For a less spicy variation, substitute the same amount of mild Italian sausage.

The recipe calls for green bell pepper, but use red, yellow, orange or a combination of any of them if that's what you have on hand.

Acknowledgments

I couldn't have written this book without the support of so many people, starting with my editor, Elizabeth Seise. Her first email asking me if I'd ever considered writing a book was the spark that ignited this whole journey and I'm so grateful for her support and guidance along the way. I feel lucky to have had the opportunity to work with her and the talented team at Page Street Publishing.

There aren't enough words to express my thanks to Kristen Schockett, Suzi Anderson, Vicki Forwood, Kaye Binning, Barb Norris, Bridget Smith and Bobby Anderson, who all wholeheartedly tested recipes and shared their thoughtful feedback, making the book better than it would have been otherwise.

Throughout the process, I made more than a few long phone calls to Lonnie and Bill Dennis, during which I talked incessantly about the book. They not only willingly picked up the phone to listen, but they also built me up with their support and words of encouragement.

And I'm forever grateful to Judy Katz, who helped me see what's possible.

About the Author

April Anderson is the creator of the blog Girl Gone Gourmet, where she creates recipes for people who love to cook comfort food–inspired dishes with simple and accessible ingredients. Her recipes have been featured on CountryLiving.com, Chowhound.com, Self.com and Buzzfeed.com, as well as other places around the Web. April lives in North Carolina with her golden retriever, Feynman.

Index